The Experience of History

The Experience of History

Kenneth Bartlett

WILEY Blackwell

This edition first published 2017

Registered Office
John Wiley & Sons, Ltd, The Atrium, Southern Gate, Chichester,
West Sussex, PO19 8SQ, UK

Editorial Offices
350 Main Street, Malden, MA 02148-5020, USA
9600 Garsington Road, Oxford, OX4 2DQ, UK
The Atrium, Southern Gate, Chichester, West Sussex, PO19 8SQ, UK

For details of our global editorial offices, for customer services, and for information about how to apply for permission to reuse the copyright material in this book please see our website at www.wiley.com/wiley-blackwell.

Library of Congress Cataloging-in-Publication Data

Names: Bartlett, Kenneth R., author.
Title: The experience of history / Kenneth Bartlett.
Description: Malden, MA : John Wiley & Sons, Inc., 2016. | Includes bibliographical references and index.
Identifiers: LCCN 2016036795 (print) | LCCN 2016042775 (ebook) | ISBN 9781118912010 (cloth) | ISBN 9781118912003 (pbk.) | ISBN 9781118911990 (pdf) | ISBN 9781118911983 (epub)
Subjects: LCSH: History–Methodology. | History–Study and teaching.
Classification: LCC D16 .B23 2016 (print) | LCC D16 (ebook) | DDC 907–dc23
LC record available at https://lccn.loc.gov/2016036795

A catalogue record for this book is available from the British Library.

Cover image: Michael Phillips/Gettyimages

Set in 10.5/13.5pt Galliard by SPi Global, Pondicherry, India

10 9 8 7 6 5 4 3 2 1

Contents

Preface

Some years ago I was occasionally visited in my office at Victoria College in the University of Toronto by an editor from Wiley-Blackwell, Tessa Harvey. She lived in Britain and worked out of the Oxford office of John Wiley & Sons but she had relatives in Toronto and consequently took advantage of the family connection to solicit authors and textbook adoptions from the faculty of my university. During these visits we talked of history as a discipline and how it had developed, what forms it took, and how its study could provide the platform for a liberal education and the skills needed in a complex world. Understanding the dynamic of the past and the causes of events are, we agreed, essential elements both in a student's preparation for life and work and in an educated citizen's understanding of how the world we live in functions. After several of these conversations, Tessa asked me to write a book on the study of history that would not be an undergraduate or upper-school textbook in the traditional sense but a consideration of history as a discipline. The idea was to produce a book that would be interesting to an educated lay audience wishing to engage with history as a means of understanding how the past served as a prologue to our own time and as an instrument for appreciating how every generation of historian recasts the evidence. I argued at the time that the study of history was an ideal way to access the perspectives of the past and assess how the present is constantly forcing a re-evaluation of what we believed happened before we were born. Although I was committed to other projects at the time, I was convinced by Tessa that this would be a worthwhile enterprise and one which would help anyone with even a cursory interest in the past to follow the contours of a notoriously fractious discipline, populated by articulate but frustratingly argumentative practitioners.

My arguments against writing this book were partly driven by the question of whether I was the best historian to attempt it. I have practised the study and teaching of history for over 30 years. I have taught every level of student from newly admitted first years in European surveys to senior graduate seminars. I have supervised doctoral theses in history and I have published a significant bibliography ranging across many aspects of the past from translations and editions to monographs and a great many articles in journals. I have spoken at a long list of academic conferences around the world and I have made educational video series and appeared on television. I am very active as a public speaker on historical subjects to groups ranging from senior alumni to dining clubs; and I lead academic tour groups, as well as teaching in my university's study abroad programmes in Europe. I have had the honour of being recognized as a fine educator, winning a great many awards for teaching, service, and scholarship. I have held administrative positions that gave me the opportunity to experiment with new means of delivering the university curriculum and establishing what that curriculum should be. My courses are both traditional – including the large, 500-student introductory survey in European history – and interdisciplinary, having taught on my college's interdisciplinary programme in Renaissance Studies since its inception.

I am providing this *cursus honorum* not to establish my credentials for writing this book but to declare that, despite this long and successful career, I am still not certain what history is and what it does; indeed, one of the reasons I agreed to write this book was to help in the process of defining my own discipline and how historians fit into it. In this voyage of discovery, I have been more successful than I thought I might be, inasmuch as I believe that I have at least raised the questions that everyone who confronts the past must address, whether first-year undergraduates or renowned scholars. The categories, skills, and methods I describe in my book do appear to have worked for me; however, as in any engagement with students of any kind, the sure knowledge that a deep and meaningful understanding of the process of historical writing and research has been transmitted remains uncertain.

The second issue, which I discussed at length with my editors, first Tessa, and after her retirement, Peter Coveney from the Boston office of Wiley, was whether a historian of the European Renaissance could bring sufficient examples and methods from other areas of research and teaching to make the book universally attractive and useful. I confessed that my own work has taken me exclusively into the study of Europe and its culture, even though I have lectured and consulted for universities in China and the Middle East, and even though my own students represent likely the most diverse student body in the world. In my large class, about half of the students were born outside Canada and speak dozens of languages from around the world at home. This, of course, merely reflects the multicultural metropolis that is Toronto; but it also reflects the interest that these diverse students take in studying Europe, particularly those who are recent immigrants or whose origins are very distant from British North America. When I meet with them, my students always say that that they are in my class because they want to understand the culture and institutions of the West, because those are the elements which will necessarily shape their lives in Canada. Even though they admit that confronting certain subjects is challenging to their own traditions, religions, and attitudes, mostly learnt from their families but still very much part of their world-view, they also affirm the importance of knowing how and why their traditions vary from those in a western, free enterprise, parliamentary democracy. This imposes a serious responsibility on me as a historian and teacher. It is heartening and humbling and requires sensitivity and openness; but it works.

Consequently, my examples in this book are almost all from Europe, from antiquity to the modern world: those are the traditions that have shaped western historical discourse and our use of evidence. And, frankly, these are the examples that I know and understand best. I learnt early from my very diverse students that to try to enter into another culture or tradition without a deep grasp of the complex forces at work within that distant civilization leads to superficial judgments and false analogies, those *faux amis* that are so glaring when a scholar moves well outside his or her own area of experience. This I honestly learnt from my students: they work hard to avoid such generalizations and shallow narratives, so I must do the same. Furthermore, in the study of history the examples and references matter less than one would expect. Of course, the sources are different and the academic practices of scholarship vary from place to place. But we are, as I note near the end of my book, all disciples of Descartes (René Descartes 1596–1650) in one way or another. Scientific method, empiricism, rigorous, honest research in primary documents, and a deep knowledge of what others have written obtain everywhere, not just in North America and not just in Renaissance European History. Nevertheless, if there are readers who expected a world vision in this book, I apologize because I am not the historian to provide it; there are others better equipped. What I am is an educator and scholar who is faced with a complex interdisciplinary area of research and who has taught students from every small corner of the planet. From them I learnt how to make my work accessible to a broad audience, and to them I am greatly indebted.

History is a particularly complex discipline because it includes almost every aspect of the human condition. It is far from the old political narrative of what happened when; now it follows the contours of our past – actually our several pasts – in such a way that the shared humanity of all of those who have gone before is revealed. I attempt to indicate the importance of this both in my discussion of what kinds of evidence survive and how that evidence should be approached and in my taxonomy of the discipline, dividing my subject into its various subcategories in a manner that might appear almost Linnaean. The purpose of this detailed analysis in the book is to witness and reinforce the wonderful explosion of new historical perspectives that have developed since the Second World War, in some instances during the past few decades. Today, there are so many ways of accessing the experience of our fellow humans in times past that no one scholar or student can ever master them all or even review them all in anything like a comprehensive way. One consequence of this is what many lay readers of history lament: the proliferation of studies that are very sharply focused on a very narrow aspect of the past. The broad sweeps that we associate either with popular history or with some of the great works of earlier scholarship are seldom seen and are even more seldom produced by professional historians. An academic wit once remarked that a professor of history is someone who knows more and more about less and less until he or she knows everything about nothing. This is, of course, a joke; but many see a grain of truth in the observation that academic historical writing appears to have left the general reader behind.

The cause of this results in part from the way in which PhD students in history are trained and their need to produce a substantial publication from the finished thesis to be competitive in a very difficult academic labour market. A broad sweeping study would not easily provide this material. But the current situation also results from our expansion of what constitutes evidence and what we consider to be important. By seeing almost every kind of survival from the past as useful documentation and by desiring a comprehensive picture of moments in the past that shed light on previously obscure spaces, historians are creating pieces of a puzzle which, when put together, reveal a much richer picture of the worlds we have lost. We now know so much more about the lives, attitudes, and circumstances of our ancestors that we should rejoice in this richness, not lament a lost golden age of accessible historical writing. That genre of popular or accessible history is still available and is often extremely well done in several media. I myself have produced video courses and appeared on television to bring an aspect of my own professional interest and knowledge to a general audience. What we see, then, is not a distancing of history from the educated wider population but a much richer choice of books, subjects, media, and interests. To complain that we are losing our sense of collective self-knowledge by not having a single, clearly formulated national or cultural narrative is to rail against the diversity and complexity of the modern world.

Certain elements in contemporary historical writing can be discordant. Some of these uncomfortable examples result from the movement of history out of the general areas of rhetoric, narrative, and traditional methodologies. We all like stories, and the etymological connections between those stories and history reveals how close they once were. Indeed, in the distant past, there was no distinction: Homer wrote poetry but also provided much of what we know about the Trojan War. Suetonius (Gaius Suetonius Tranquillus, *c.* 69–after 122 AD) wrote gossip about the first 12 Roman emperors in a way that would not be inappropriate for supermarket tabloids; but, again, we have derived much important evidence from his observations. What we demand now, however, is not just a good story in poetry or prose but a fair and engaging assessment of a piece of our history which we can accept as reliable because of the rigorous use of evidence and analysis. The historian remains an important part of this exercise because it is she or he who puts the pieces together and draws conclusions from them. It is still the historian who speaks, not the evidence: in every good historian a bit of Homer and Suetonius lives. Evidence and documentation, as well as the received scholarship on the question, are passive, inert materials that require a historian to assemble them into a critical mass so that some kind of intellectual fission will occur. It is for this reason that I offer a chapter on the historian and privilege him or her over the materials he or she uses.

I do not let the historian off completely, however, from certain charges against the profession. There is never need for jargon or impenetrable language. If an interdisciplinary study of the past employs the language of another discipline, it should be explained and domesticated into plain, clear, effective speech. Levels of diction can remain high, as a memory of the fact that history was once a branch of rhetoric; but a sophisticated vocabulary is not the same as the precious speech of those scholars who want to limit their audiences to those who share their perspectives. This tendency to use jargon really proves Freud's (Sigismund Freud, 1856–1939) observation about the narcissism of small differences. Language should be welcoming and inclusive, not a barrier to general understanding.

Finally, I would like to affirm my own belief in the efficacy of reading, studying, and writing history. It is an exacting discipline, but one which brings together every aspect of our knowledge and experience. To study history is to study the whole development of entire civilizations, even if only a small part at a time. The complexity of the human condition, the almost numberless forces at work on every society, and the actions that result from either careful or headlong decisions require a subtle and deep appreciation of what it is to be human, living in a community and balancing the public and private good. I tell my students that very few of them will graduate and find work as professional historians; but every one of them will be historians in that their training will give them the skills and knowledge to navigate a demanding and difficult world. To know how others have reacted to crisis or opportunity is to assist in the decisions that every citizen must make for him or herself, in the family, the community, the nation, and the world. To read or hear the news with a deeper understanding, or to cast a vote for a political candidate based on a more profound appreciation of the issues at stake is to validate the study of history. To see others – wherever and whenever they are encountered – as part of a common humanity or as fellow travellers on the shared paths of the human condition is to apply the lessons of history. When the Roman playwright Terence (Publius Terentius Afer, *c.* 195–*c.* 159 BC) wrote that 'I am human, so nothing human should be alien to me', he was stating the reason we study history, and why were are fortunate that there are now so many aspects to historical study that few elements of our humanity are excluded.

There are many people who contributed to the writing of this book, some actively and others unknowingly. In the former category, I mention and again, with sincere appreciation, Tessa Harvey, whose gentle intensity convinced me to embark on the work, Peter Coveney, who assumed Tessa's role after her retirement and who has proved an insightful and rigorous reader, and finally Brian Stone who replaced Peter after his retirement. Then, as always, there is my wife, Gillian, my sharpest critic and most trusted editor. In the latter category I include all of my students, from first year to my PhD students, many of whom are now teaching history at other universities across the continent. These outstanding young people have forced me to constantly evaluate and re-evaluate what I am saying and writing, and their rich diversity has shown me how important the concept of universal human principles and careful judgments are in teaching and research. Finally, my many colleagues in a great many disciplines over a long period of time deserve recognition. We have not always agreed professionally but the disagreements have for the most part been open and respectful discussions about varying interpretations of the past. You have brought so much of your own knowledge and wit to our formal and informal debates about history that I am much the richer for having heard your arguments and read your work.

My sincere hope is that this book will be used by students at every level and by anyone interested in navigating the modern practice of history. It is written to be provocative and as comprehensive as possible, given the limitations of its author. It acknowledges that there are a great many other ways of approaching the reading, writing, and assessing of history; thus any entry into history requires a guide, or in the world of contemporary technology, a GPS. That is what I hope this book offers.

Kenneth Bartlett
Victoria College
University of Toronto

1

Introduction

The American industrialist, Henry Ford, once famously said that history is bunk. Although he fortunately changed his opinion, he was speaking for a number of those who saw the past as irrelevant or at best an antiquarian interest in the silent, if entertaining, dead. This opinion did not die with him. Recently, a financial guru has said that the past can teach us nothing, that everything worthwhile should come from the file 'going forward'. For his highly lucrative profession, then, his advice was to ignore what went before and concentrate on what was to come. I could, of course, provide a great many more quotes and examples. Or, I could counter each and every one with an opposite observation praising the value of studying history made by scholars and politicians of the stature of the ancient Roman statesman Cicero (*d.* 43 BC) or the modern British Prime Minister, Winston Churchill (*d.* 1965). But, to those who see little value in history, this would just be testimony from those same irrelevant, dead advocates of an essentially useless discipline.

So, why study history, if there is a debate as to whether it is of any use in the modern world? And, if it is useful, where exactly is its value to be found? How can we gain significance and guidance from what happened before we were born or in distant lands so different from our own? The answers to these questions and the brief in favour of the study of history are what this book is about. To be sure, the past is a foreign country but one not only worth visiting, but instructive,

The Experience of History, First Edition. Kenneth Bartlett.

insightful, and useful. The experience of the past and what men and women have made of those experiences subsequently constitute the record of human civilization and the platform on which our modern world is built. To ignore or disparage this journey through time, this desire to see the past through modern eyes, is to miss an opportunity to give nuance and explanation to not only what happened before we were born but more urgently to the universe we are inhabiting at this very moment. Also, the trajectory of the past can provide clues to the unfolding of the future. I am not saying that history repeats itself; but it does, if used skilfully, reveal patterns and motives that can inform our own decisions. So, to the financial guru, I would counter that he is simply wrong: he has chosen to ignore one of the most effective guides to success in his profession. Financial markets and the global economy are driven by people. Any deeper insight we can gather into what drives people to make the choices they do, favour one product over another, embrace or reject the foreign and exotic or simply aspire to something different or new is more than useful: it is necessary.

Another argument thrown against studying history is that historians seem unable to agree on anything, that they use the past as ammunition in wars that have not much to do with what might have occurred long ago but have much to say about the current state of our own world. In other words, history is rewritten to justify the failures or ambitions of those who write it and those who read it. Well, I could not agree more: this is exactly what results from the study of historiography (the formal study of written history over time as a discipline). And, it is a good thing. Let me explain.

To have any relevance or validity, the past must speak to the needs and concerns of the present and future. Consequently, as those imperatives change with time, location, ideology or prejudice, the view of the past will change as well. This is what makes history a dynamic, vital, and living discipline. It will always be current and its interpretation accordingly changes with its environment. There is something almost evolutionary in the way in which history adapts to the environment in which it is written. And, as with surviving species, the most adaptable and the strongest – at least in terms of evidence and argument – will endure. These surviving historical interpretations will always be challenged by new, even more adaptable and effective interpretations; and some of the dominant schools of historical thought that had lasted for generations, even centuries, will eventually be discarded as no longer useful. That is the glory and strength of history: the fact that it is always in a state of flux, changing and alive. The past is not dead because those who study and interpret the past are very much alive.

What then about 'facts', those dates, events, reigns, wars, elections, victories, and defeats that are often the popular definition of historical research? They exist, that I concede. But in themselves they have little utility or value. They are simply records of particular moments on which most students and historians agree, with appropriate evidence to substantiate this belief. But, these 'facts of history' have no purpose and use beyond how they are interpreted, what they meant at the time and afterwards, and what they mean to us. These 'facts' are like pegs on a wall: they are useful for hanging deeper study and analysis. To know these 'facts' is convenient, as they provide a logical chronology and structure for understanding the past. And, they serve as a generally accepted vocabulary in the discourse among historians. What matters, then, is not the 'facts' but how these operate as evidence, as points of agreement or departure, elements of structure and design.

In this book we will talk a great deal about evidence, including 'facts', that is, evidence which is broadly accepted and substantiated by documents or records. But, we will also argue that the interpretation of this evidence matters far more and that even our assessment of 'facts' changes. Let me give you an example: for millennia the study of history was structured according to theological 'facts', evidence that emerged from the revealed texts of faith, such as the Bible or the Koran. No one in the cultures that produced these histories would ever have disputed the fundamental truth of these 'facts'. But, after the Renaissance and Enlightenment in Europe, and certainly today, hardly anyone, whether a professional historian or not, would accept these religious 'facts' as valid evidence of what happened to real men and women eons ago, even if they can indeed offer clues. So, everything can change, including fundamental ideas or structures that have guided historians for centuries.

That is not to say that even such traditional and now outmoded structures have been altogether thrown into the dustbin of history. Just look at how we measure the passage of time itself. In the Christian world, the past is divided by the letters BC or AD, that, is Before Christ and Anno Domini, that is, in Latin, in the year of our Lord. The incarnation, then, becomes the most significant element in recording time and bisects Christian history. Similarly, Muslims date the past from the Christian year 672 AD, that is, the year of the *Hajira*, when Mohammad fled from Mecca to Medina. Thus, 2015 is the year 1343. Jews record time from the creation of the first man and woman, Adam and Eve, as described in Genesis; and the year begins on that day. So, in the Hebrew calendar, 2015 is the year 5775. I should note, though, that in the secular west there is now an attempt to negate the Christian associations of BC and AD by replacing these religiously structured terms with BCE – or Before Common Era – and CE, or Common Era. The concept of Common Era would, however, be lost on Muslims and Jews who retain their own dating and do not necessarily see the past as 'Common'.

The study of history has often been defined as the study of change over time. And, historians change, too, as does acceptable evidence. Thus, things we completely accept, indeed privilege, had little or no purchase among the historians of the past. Economic History hardly existed at all until quite recently; Social History was either curious antiquarianism or ignored until about the same time. Women's History came into its own as a respected sub-discipline just in the last century and Queer History is now just developing into an effective and recognized genre of its own. The documents, evidence, insights, and texts used by these branches of history were certainly available and known previously, but they were only identified as valid, useful, and in fact necessary when the society of those writing and reading history realized that these perspectives added important aspects to our understanding both of the past and the present. These sub-disciplines became the instruments for illuminating what had been before the dark corners of human experience and they gave a powerful and effective voice to those whose pasts had been ignored or even unjustly vilified. As a result we are all much richer and the experience of being human in a complex and diverse world is greatly expanded.

We are All Part of the Evidence

Later in this book, in the chapter on evidence, I note that documents from what amounts to daily life constitute essential evidence from the past, evidence that the historian might use to fashion a set of carefully crafted conclusions about the society that created these documents and the individuals and groups who inhabit them. Census records, taxation rolls, property deeds, judicial, and official government files, and so many other tesserae in the mosaic of the lives and communities of those who went before us remain among the most important evidentiary platforms on which history is constructed. Consider our own lives. Think of the documents we sign and file every year, almost every day. There are the important ones that we conserve in a safe or a secure drawer in a desk, often with duplicates kept in lawyers' offices or bank vaults: birth certificates, marriage licences, college or university diplomas, property deeds or rental leases, and wills, just to note the most common. These are the same documents that historians have used to discover the contours of past societies; so, we are saving the evidence for tomorrow's history.

Consider as well the intimate and personal material that every one of us keeps, often in places more secure than those protecting our legal and financial personae. Love letters, diaries, correspondence through a war or unwanted separation, photographs, home movies, cards, newspaper clippings celebrating personal or family achievements, a marriage or birth, or an obituary, or just something that spoke to you in an intimate manner. We keep letters offering employment, personal notes from employers, co-workers, neighbours or friends, or just something that reflects an act of personal connection or kindness. Then, there are the negative categories: letters of rejection – of us or a manuscript – a notice of termination of employment, accusatory correspondence from the local troublemaker, taxation office interrogatories or a warning of legal proceedings. These are kept as well either as protection against future loss or as a record of a clouded time. Here again, we are conserving the evidence that social historians find invaluable, as it records the details of a life in our community at a particular moment.

Finally, go outside the home and think of the enormous body of evidence about our lives that exists in government files at every level, in our place of work, in the clubs we belong to, in the agencies we support and the political parties and candidates we assist through volunteering or financial contributions. Moreover, what letters or documents of ours are our neighbours conserving? Are the love letters or even friendly correspondence we wrote over many years part of another's cache of carefully preserved material? Often, the author of evidence is not even aware that it is being preserved. When reading biographies or history, how often are we told that only one side of an important exchange of correspondence survives? This happens often enough to suggest perhaps that one of the interlocutors intended that the nature of the exchange remain secret while the other thought it worth preserving.

We are all, then, part of the historical record. Some of us aggressively use this material for personal reasons, such as genealogical research. Indeed, the explosion in the interest in genealogy has turned a great number of curious individuals into quite skilled historians, familiar with census records, passenger ship manifests, birth, death, and military records, newspaper obituaries and notices of births and marriages. Entire websites now exist to assist amateur genealogists, organized by family name, or sometimes determined by place, all rich in shared information based upon reliable evidence. What this growing interest in genealogy reveals is the almost obsessive fascination about where we came from, who our ancestors were and where we sit on this revolving carousel of time. We have a truly anthropological interest in our roots, the back story of our lives. This is how history becomes not an academic discipline but part of a personal narrative, a connection that brings the study of the past home. Most of us have spent hours looking through a grandparent's photograph album, trying to gather insight about an entire *dramatis personae* of times past, inhabited by people we never met or even knew existed. The excitement felt in confronting this reality of our own pasts has created a great many historians, both amateur and professional. We all want to know where **we** are placed in the parade of the ages and how we were assigned that place. It is natural and it is why history sustains a popular fascination that so many other disciplines do not.

A Personal Example

It is not even necessary to recognize those from the past you encounter in daily life. Strangers long dead can exert an attraction born out of some small point of shared experience. Let me give you an example from my own life. Our house is just over a century old but was occupied by two generations of the same family from the 1920s until we acquired it in 1988. The family line had ended with the death of the last elderly unmarried daughter, who had grown up in the house; and it was from her estate we bought the property. We had heard a great many stories and legends about this rather eccentric, once wealthy but later shabby genteel clan from friends and neighbours in the street: how the previous owner's father had been killed in a famous British train crash in the early twentieth century; how his widow believed she was poor because all widows were poor; and how she raised her three young children as if they were still living in Victorian times, protecting them, she thought, by discouraging marriages and most professions, resulting in the end of what was a very old, distinguished family. We knew that they treated the household staff they maintained until the end very badly. The service staircase was not illuminated at all, leaving it completely dark when the doors at either end were closed. The elderly spinster who became the last scion of this clan boasted that she had never as much as washed a teacup in her life; and this was confirmed by a kitchen that was a time capsule from the 1920s, with only a single overhead bulb for light and appliances that had not been replaced in decades. The service bells throughout the house still worked; sadly, when pressed now, no one comes.

These legends and stories created an almost Faulknerian atmosphere for us, and the physical evidence of the house reinforced it to a very great degree. But was there more? Of course, the former owners of our house were people, with lives and emotions and stories. They were very much unlike us; but they were also interesting representatives of their time, class, and breeding. In fact, the house was an entrée into a more layered past, a society now thankfully passed. Our lives overlapped, but they seemed so much like exiles from that other country which was the past; because their lives were so remote and inflexible they almost succeeded in making time stand still: hence their fascination for me as a historian. Trying to know the last members of this old, extinct family became a subject of desultory and unprofessional but consuming interest. Small pieces of evidence began to emerge that linked the material history of the house and the few objects we found in it with the real human beings who had inhabited it for so long.

At a dinner party, a very old gentleman reminisced how he had long ago in his youth courted the last inhabitant, the never married daughter. He remembered that she had been a wonderful dancing companion in the 1930s, one who loved a party – hardly what we were told of her when she was in her 80s and living like a semi-recluse attended by an elderly maid and revolving nurses. But, at the very back of an upstairs closet we had discovered a decaying evening dress, beautifully made, with weights in the skirts to maintain modesty when dancing, as well as in strong winds. The dancing story gained more credence, as the material evidence of the dress reinforced the oral history. Then, a very elderly neighbour confessed to having visited the old lady every Friday afternoon for decades, a meeting where they would consume much scotch and gossip about mutual friends: she remarked that the old spinster had a wicked tongue, reactionary values, but a keen mind.

By coincidence, the lawyer who had represented the family, as his father had before him – indeed the lawyer who had arranged the conveyance of the property – was an acquaintance of ours. We learnt of the sad family history, the accidental death of the very successful and distinguished father at a relatively young age and the devastation that resulted, as his widow was left with three young children and the responsibility to care for them, despite her previously never having any control of finances or much knowledge of the world. Our florist had been the family's florist and the very elderly owner remarked often how the widow in trying to protect the children had infantilized them – and so it went. What was discovered in small bits and pieces was the history of a house, the family that occupied it for a great many years and how all of these elements came together as a picture of a society.

More personal information emerged as a result of the kinds of accidents that occur when doing renovations. In the library of the house, the surround of the fireplace had to be removed in order to rewire and repair the walls. Behind the mantle was found a cache of cards that had fallen through a space left after it had become slightly detached from the wall sometime in 1933 but had subsequently been repaired. The cards found in the wall all dated from the winter of 1933 and had obviously been placed on the mantle as reminders. There were notices of dental appointments, several Christmas cards, and birthday greetings. All had been sent to the second son, Philip, who we learnt was universally called 'Pip'. In themselves, these were ephemera only; but in the context of the emerging history of the house and family they were significant because the individuals were very much brought to life: these were real people with dental appointments, friends, and birthdays; they celebrated Christmas and used the library mantle to display current invitations and greetings – and at least one had a nickname.

A source of melancholy, an emotion which all historians have felt with some regularity, was the loss of the family's photograph albums. Our lawyer acquaintance, whose firm had arranged the emptying of the house, told us that there were dozens of them which traced visually the history of the family in the house. He confessed to a sense of guilt at having thrown them out because no one wanted them; and he admitted that had he known that I, a historian, was buying the house, he would have passed them along. His fleeting memory of what those albums contained was devastating to my desire to recover the past life of our house, as the photos depicted the furniture in place during the previous half century, the few changes made to the décor and fabric of the building, and the aging of the inhabitants, as they were portrayed over that long span in rooms where almost nothing changed. I have no idea what any of these people, whose home and personalities I feel I know so well, looked like.

As a historian, however, I also know that my assumption that I do know them is completely false. I do know things about them, based on evidence which in some instances is reliable – like written documents – and in others very unreliable, like the recollection of neighbours who only knew them as old, difficult, querulous, and demanding people, trying to live like Edwardian gentry with a single octogenarian housemaid in a house that, to quote the lawyer, 'had not heard laughter in a great many years'. What I also know is that my past and present have become linked with those of the previous owners, although I am equally aware, as a professional, that my response is more romantic than scientific. What this personal testament records, then, is evidence for a very obvious conclusion: we are all living in history, contributing to the evidence of the future while being in a constant, and intimate, conversation with the dead around us. It is for this reason that I felt a somewhat comforting sense of closure when I discovered their shared family grave and monument in a downtown cemetery.

What I am describing is that mixture of material culture – that is, the evidence in the house itself and things found inside it – written documentation both of a highly personal and an official nature, and a rich oral history and local tradition that constitutes the very elements that define much of historical research. Add to it the circumstances of the tragic death of the father, whose end in a dramatic disaster was reported widely in newspapers throughout England, Canada, and the United States from New York to Los Angeles, and a relatively coherent narrative emerges, one with a beginning and an end. These were substantial citizens with property and social standing, as well as the fossilized habits of the colonial gentry; but they were also characters in a history that continues. My wife and I now live in their house, and there are still some elderly neighbours who remember them. The house would be in many ways still recognizable to them, as the fine detailing was preserved, and most of the rooms function as they did then; but, at the same time, the house today would be shocking, with many more bathrooms, a kitchen addition in which we do the work without the benefit of a maid to wash teacups, and with mechanical services expected of a modern house. So, are we living in history? Of course, we all do, regardless where and when we live: history is everywhere and it is the prologue to our own personal and collective narratives. We make history every day and all our records will without doubt be included in some future analysis of North America in the twenty-first century.

History is not a thing apart, about someone else, somewhere else, in another time: it is our daily regime, which has been determined by the decisions and deeds of generations who came before us. And, if at any moment, we feel a twinge of identification with the circumstances of someone from the past, or find ourselves sufficiently curious to want to know more about why things are the way they are – as I did with my house – or just experience a *frisson* of excitement when discovering new information about anything or anyone who is no longer here to witness for it, then we are doing history and we are all historians.

Still, the past is a foreign country and not one easily visited. We need good maps and that universal GPS to guide us through the experience of other men and women, long dead, who can no longer speak for themselves. We need to give these people their voices in a language we can clearly understand so that they can advise us on how we might improve, direct, and even save our own world and leave it better understood for future generations. This book will provide the coordinates of that GPS, offer a guide to how to navigate the challenging terrain of the past. The skills required are the skills of a successful life and career:

the ability to read effectively and write clearly, evaluate evidence, and draw conclusions, build arguments and establish priorities in research. The rewards are naturally great because the student of history will not only acquire and polish these skills but be an active, engaged, and knowledgeable member of his or her society, able to understand the intentions and schemes of others, critique the official sources of information, political platforms, and personal aspirations. And, the study of history will allow each and every one of us to understand why things are the way they are, how the world might be improved, what has worked in the past and what has not, and what the future can be like, if certain decisions are made and conditions apply. History, then, is the study of humanity, of ourselves or our past – our respective pasts – the pasts that made us who we are.

2

The Historian not the History

History was not only made by people; it was written and hence to a degree remade by people. Events in the past have no validity except for the significance that we subsequently assign to them; so in reality the study of history is the study of historians. As a result, it is necessary to put the history you read into the context of the person who wrote it. Determining who he or she was, when the history or document was composed, for whom it was written and the general intellectual and cultural environment of the author will provide a necessary insight into how you should interpret what is delivered on the page as 'fact' or judge the validity of the conclusions.

To do this, first discover the nature of the individual who has written what is described as history. If the historian is writing at the request of a powerful individual or a government, you need to question how many negative elements are suppressed in order to allow the positive parts of the narrative to shine. So you must ask how distant the historian was from his or her sources and the events or situation studied. In instances of sponsorship, commissions, or dedications, this is not usually very difficult. But, there are more subtle aspects of this tainting of the judgment of the historian. Let's imagine that the author of a history was once a member of a particular political party in government, or served a royal court or worked for a certain individual or company as an official. Can you uncritically accept the conclusions such a historian has provided? This operates, moreover, both positively and

The Experience of History, First Edition. Kenneth Bartlett.

negatively. The historian might want to praise or exculpate the deeds or decisions of a king, administration, or individual; but he or she might equally want to damage their reputations to repay a slight, justify a personal failure, or even dismissal. It has been said that the memoirs of most politicians written when out of office are studies of how and why they lost their jobs. What I think you will find is that this is an accurate observation in a great many cases.

Besides the professional bias that can arise when a historian writes about an agency or institution of which he or she was once a part, we should look at the larger question of ideological, philosophical, or religious bias. For example, during the Cold War, can we assume that an American and a Russian historian would draw similar conclusions from the same event, even if they used identical evidence? Or, would a Muslim or Jewish historian see the 1492 expulsion of the Muslims and Jews from Spain in the same way a Spanish Catholic might? This is not to say that all historians pervert evidence to service their ideologies, careers, or religions: it merely suggests that historical narratives can be driven by considerations outside the pure analysis of documents, sources, and events – often unconsciously.

To a substantial degree what we know about the past and how we frame that knowledge is the result of what others have written. Historiography is the received collective insight of those who have written about the past and the cumulative results of their research; but it is hardly a coherent, linear, or comprehensive analysis. It is formed by the perspective and the experience of the historian and as a consequence needs to be read critically to tease out his or her biases and assumptions. Often, indeed normally, these are unstated and occasionally not even consciously recognized by the historian. We all work in the context of our times, the prevailing values and structure of our societies, and the normal practices of our profession, so this context must be understood in order to evaluate the work of every writer of history. Moreover, the heavy weight of the cumulative scholarship of entire historical traditions, cultural and intellectual environments, and immediate circumstances all should be unpacked to reveal the assumptions of any school or generation of historians. The great many texts that taken together comprise the historiography of any time or place have a powerful momentum that can overwhelm even the most sceptical student or reader. If many historians agree or use the same methodology or sources, you should not simply assume that their conclusions are valid. All historians build on the work of others and none writes in a scholarly or cultural vacuum: a prudent scepticism and careful reading are necessary to offer fresh perspectives or at least escape the chains of received interpretations or prescriptive methods.

Ideological History

Let's look, for example, at the role of ideology in history. A Marxist will use a particular structure of analysis in writing history. Generally, this will affirm the Marxist operation of history as the theatre of economic or class divisions and conflict. The capitalist thesis in such a study will always be challenged by the proletarian antithesis and will assume the ultimate victory of socialism. Few Marxist historians today are as unreconstructed as to follow without deviation a pure Marxist analysis, or so it would appear. Yet, beneath the surface of these scholars' works will often be found the unstated or assumed belief in the final victory of socialism and the demise of capitalism and capitalists, the necessary consequence of their 'internal contradictions'. There is almost invariably a sense of teleology, that is, history unfolding for a purpose; and there is always a belief in 'progress': that is, history is a journey towards a better and fairer world. It is often not difficult to identify heroes and victims in this analysis and to see how the ideological framework determines the choice of events and evidence. All historians engage in this selective process, even if only through the heavier weight of a particular form of evidence or interpretation.

The same can be said of those historians whose ideologies are different but equally selective. During the Cold War it would have been difficult to find many historians in the United States, for example, who would praise the Soviet Union, the regime of Stalin (1878–1953) or Mao Tse Tung (1893–1976), or the Soviet hegemony in Eastern Europe. Partly this results from legitimate belief and part of it comes from the experience of those writing in the 1950s and 1960s when historians reaching maturity would have been conditioned by their education and ambient intellectual environment. But, some of it also comes from the recognition that support of these general values was necessary for a successful career. Even if protected by tenure in a university, writing history in ways that conflict with the general ideology and official policy of established authority can potentially compromise his or her professional reputation. This applies in relatively open liberal democracies as well as totalitarian states where information is censored and controlled. To be seen to apologize for the 'enemy' in even a cold war or to appear disloyal or even treacherous would have made the publication of scholarly work more difficult, result in conflict with the hierarchy of the historian's school, university, or employer and even occasion his or her ostracism from mainstream historical debate. Although the consequences of not 'towing the party line' were much more onerous in the Soviet or communist camp, there were also pressures in the west as well. So, regardless where a historical study was published or written, you need to look into the ideological environment in which it was produced.

Much the same can be said about the broader philosophical discussion in which a historian works. During the nineteenth century there was a general belief in progress, that is, the continual improvement of the human condition in every way: economic, political, social, and personal. This produced what has often been called Whig History, a tradition that arose in liberal European states in the nineteenth and early twentieth centuries that stressed those events or ideas that were interpreted as moving history forward, propelling human civilization further into democracy, prosperity, and freedom. This was a powerful agent in Britain especially. Events were interpreted according to how they contributed to progress. Consequently, historical moments such the 1215 signing of the Magna Carta, or the summoning of the first parliament (by Simon de Montfort in 1265), or the Reformation or the defeat of Stuart absolutist tendencies in the English Civil War (1642–51) and the Glorious Revolution (1688), or the defeat of Napoleon (Waterloo 1815) as well as the extension of the franchise all were celebrated as engines of positive change. And, those opposing ideas, individuals or forces were thus characterized as contrary to progress, regressive, even evil or wrong. This kind of history identified winners and losers and operated very much as an apology for liberal nineteenth- and early twentieth-century values which were seen as the fruits, the rewards of this sequence of progressive events.

Recognizing this mentality in Whig History helps explain something that modern historians and students find reprehensible: imperial expansion and concepts of racial or national superiority. Looking at this traditional Whig perspective, the British, or the French or Belgians or any other imperial power were not only permitted to capture the lands and treasures of other peoples far distant on other continents but were almost required to do so. Imperialism brought 'progress' to these peoples, gave them access to the long and positive experiences of these colonial powers, and prepared them for one day maturing into nations modelled on their colonial masters. The institutions and technologies were the instruments of this 'civilizing mission', as the French called it; but the model and experiences of the colonial power was a guide to what the colonized peoples should want to achieve. To a modern reader this notion is reprehensible in the extreme and presupposes a sense of moral and cultural superiority that is not based on any legitimate truth. However, to understand fully a nineteenth-century historian, especially if writing about empire and exploration, this concept of the 'white man's burden' has to be understood.

This last example leads to another difficult point. It is easy to simply dismiss those historians writing in the past who worked from a set of values we now rightly deplore. Nevertheless, we must read them and do so with some knowledge of the environment in which they wrote. First, there is often useful information in these books: we do not have to share the historian's conclusions to discover useful information. Second, these works are important in entering the mind of the period in which the history was written. If we in our modern world wish to address the errors and even crimes of the past we need to understand the atmosphere in which they were committed. Simply to make a value judgment, rejecting everything written in the past that does not conform to our current ideological or moral perspective, is a mistake. If we want to ensure that such attitudes and events do not resurface to rehearse the mistakes of the past, we have to know how they arose and what ideas informed them. So, then, you do not have to admire, celebrate, or even like historians who justified or benignly described injustice; but we do have to read them.

What about more subtle clouding of evidence as a result of the experience or circumstances of the historian? If a privileged upper-class male writes about the conditions of working-class women, are we to accept his conclusions without question? This element of 'blinkered vision' in no way necessarily attributes prejudice or animosity. It merely drives every reader to ask whether the experience of someone so different from that of the historian can truly be understood. What might appear to the privileged historian is that certain labour practices or legitimate concern by factory owners for female workers were progressive; however, such liberal policies might equally be interpreted by those very working-class women or their supporters as patronizing and insufficient: really attempts to block wider political action or social legislation. Thus, the kindness and concern on the part of privileged groups could easily then be seen negatively by historians closer in experience to the subject than by those closer to the perspective and world view of the privileged historian.

Ethnic or National History

The ethnic, national, or geographic origin of the historian should also been taken into account, especially in areas where ethnic strife or civil war is concerned. Would a Serb historian mirror the observations and conclusions of a Croatian historian writing about the same events after the disintegration of the former Yugoslavia in the 1990s, even if they were both involved in the events of that crisis and had access to the same evidence? It is highly unlikely. Similarly, a Polish, Russian, German, Lithuanian, or Ukrainian historian all studying the territory presently occupied by the republic of Poland would probably produce very different kinds of histories. What I am saying is that knowing where the historian is coming from will often provide important insight into where his or her historical analysis is going. We are all products of our times, groups, and experiences. We all claim to be dispassionate, fair, and even-handed observers; but are we? Can a historian ever fully divest him or herself from the often unconscious limitations of his or her personal situations? Can any writer of history ever be truly objective?

Looking at this problem more generally, to what extent can a male historian writing Women's History be seen as authoritative? What about race? Can a white historian discuss black slavery as effectively as a black man or woman? What about a police official writing about criminal behaviour, or a jailed offender offering views on the penal system? These are not easy answers and my advice is not to make blanket judgments but to assess each example on its own terms. I have already indicated that it is necessary to take the circumstances of the historian into account; but how you do that and the degree to which you factor in the often unstated bias of the source is a judgment call you will have to make each and every time you open a history book or even use a historical document.

Distant Voices

If the historian as an individual often colours the kind of conclusions or observations he or she makes, what about the passage of time? It is reasonable to assume that describing or analysing events that occurred long ago should reduce the effect of these influences on the historian. How can, for example, a discussion of the late Roman Empire be tainted by a modern historian's circumstances? One would think the passage of 1600 or 1700 years would dilute any potential bias. But, the role of religion and even national perspective might still obtain. For example, a devout Christian would likely celebrate the imposition of Christianity as the singular official religion of late Rome and cheer the legal proscription of paganism. However, the destruction of pagan temples and art should be mourned, as much beauty and profound human experience were expunged. Should centuries of historians in the past have referred to the Germanic tribes that invaded the Roman Empire as barbarians? What does barbarian mean and to whom? The Romans and Renaissance European historians might well have called them that, but what does the term mean to us? Was our connotation theirs and is there still a value judgment in rehearsing the fall of ancient Rome as the coming of the so-called 'Dark Ages'?

And what about evidence produced in the very distant past? Distance tends to dilute even the most powerful bias but not always. Passions often cool but historical ideology remains. Also, this distancing can lead ironically to an even greater interjection of the historian's personal perspective into his or her analysis of the past. As we move farther back into the past, the evidence generally becomes scantier and often survives in unique, limited, or non-continuous series or archives. And, of course, the more distant the experience of our sources the less we can truly establish about their context, authorship, authority, or even validity. This leaves a much wider role for interpretation and indeed interpolation.

Where there are gaps or ambiguities there is consequently more opportunity for the historian to fill or rationalize them according to his or her own values, principles, ideologies, or intentions. In other words, it can often be easier for the distant past to serve the needs of the present historian by establishing precedents, preconditions, parallels, or platforms on which to build a more coherent longitudinal analysis of the events that shaped the past. All historians do this to a degree and it is essential in making sense of a world long gone and the records of people long dead and societies much changed or even forgotten. It is part of the historian's method. But it can also be dangerous, as sweeping generalizations or attributions of causality can lead to specious conclusions and results. So, as with everything else about the historian's intention to explicate the past, we must exercise caution and ask what intentions the modern writer hoped to achieve with the work. We need to be aware that modern debates evidenced by material or experiences long passed can have very questionable implications.

The most obvious examples of this result from historians imposing modern concepts of societies that not only did not use these terms but would fail to comprehend them in any way. For example, the attempt to interject nineteenth- or twentieth-century concepts of social or economic class on the Middle Ages would obviously be a very imperfect way of understanding medieval society. Medieval people and those who recorded their experience simply did not think in those terms. To be sure, there were powerful and almost universal ideas of 'degree', status, 'condition', or 'estate'; but these categories in no way functioned like, for instance, the Marxist construct of 'class'. Even prevailing concepts like faith or religion meant different things, depending on the confessional belief itself, where it was practised and who was describing the experience. So, to talk about religion in the pagan ancient world requires a different perspective on the part of the historian from, for example, a historian writing about contemporary non-monotheistic faiths, like Hinduism. Furthermore, what might seem to a modern scientific mind as superstition might well have been seen as reasonable belief and an integral part of a belief structure. And, finally, as religion operates in the realm of the supernatural by definition, earlier societies explained natural phenomena through the vocabulary of religion, attributing cause to a deity or another supernatural force simply because they did not have the tools yet for a scientific or rational explanation. This in no way defines them as primitive; it merely discusses their culture in its own terms, not ours. We all when reading history must try to see the past through the eyes of our subjects not our readers.

Thus, it is important not to attribute negative, patronizing, or infantilizing interpretations to those who lived long ago. Historians who subscribe to the belief in progress largely see science as the engine of that change in human affairs leading to the modern, rational, scientific, progressive world. This relegation of elements of past human experience to a pit of ignorance from which we have fortunately emerged, or the application of loaded terms such as primitive, unsophisticated, superstitious, or ignorant reveal more about the perspective of the historian than his or her subjects. When reading histories written, for example, in the Enlightenment or the nineteenth century these historical prejudices become clear. And, it is our obligation to take these attitudes into account when judging the validity of such historical studies.

Historical Style or Genre

Can the style or genre of historical writing tell us much about the historian and the context of his or her work? History in the ancient world and Renaissance was seen as a branch of rhetoric; thus, style mattered just as much as content. Ancient Roman historians, such as Livy (Titus Livius Patavinus, *c.* 59 BC–17 AD) concocted imaginary speeches and placed these into the mouths of historical figures, such as the Carthaginian general Hannibal (Hannibal Barca, *c.* 247–*c.* 181 BC), to give his historical narrative some energy and immediacy. This rhetorical style was adopted in the Renaissance, leading even those early founders of modern historical method, such as Leonardo Bruni (*c.* 1370–1444) in fifteenth-century Florence, to adopt this style. Bruni might have been a pioneer in the use of primary sources and the evaluation of evidence but he was also a man of his times, that of Renaissance humanism, in which style was as important as the content. It was believed that history was a collection of examples of good and bad practice and consequently could serve as a guide to the contemporary world. And, it was believed that the desire – and ability – to follow these precepts was strengthened by the quality of the rhetorical style because it helped convince the reader what was the ethical, correct, and judicious decision, modelled on ancient examples. Style also helped the reader remember the passage; and the very human quality of recording an almost theatrical recreation of events served the ethical purpose history was expected to exemplify. Today, of course, we believe none of this. No modern historian would write speeches for ancient heroes, such as Hannibal or Scipio Africanus (Publius Cornelius Scipio Africanus, 236 BC–183 BC), or Florentine Renaissance magistrates and insert them as if quoting a reliable document. That element has long passed; but we need to understand that it once served the historians' purpose, at least the rhetorical and ethical purpose of the classical or Renaissance historian.

But, do modern historians follow similar practices, just using different kinds of tools? Let me give you an example: if you leaf through two history texts, one heavily reliant on tables, graphs, and numerical evidence, do you think it more valid and authoritative that one written in continuous expository prose? Usually students do, because graphs and charts and numbers all seem so scientific. Numbers, you say, don't lie, so the conclusions of the historian reliant on them must be necessarily more correct. Why would you think this? The historian is the author who chooses, manipulates, and interprets those numbers; and the graphs are charts of his or her own creation. Numbers do not make history scientific: they are only different kinds of evidence used, like legal documents or diaries, to prove the historian's contentions. Numbers are just as prone to manipulation or misuse; and, when dealing with the past, historians are often at a significant disadvantage when writing quantitative history because the sources vary in detail or in reliability or longitudinal or latitudinal survival. So, ask yourself when facing a quantitative analysis of a historical period or event, how large is the historian's sample? Who collected these statistics and for what purpose; and is his or her method of using these numerical arguments sound? Numbers tend to look convincing but they are only useful or valid if prudently, carefully, and effectively used by the historian.

The Older Historian

Does the age or personal profile of the historian affect his or her analysis of the past? That is, does an older scholar, near the end of a distinguished career, have more authority than a young historian producing his or her first book? This is difficult to answer because so many factors must be considered. A historian in his or her 60s, for example, will have enjoyed a lifetime of scholarship, familiarity with evidence, and accumulated skill in analysis. The collective knowledge of decades of work and reading, of speaking at conferences to test ideas and reading reviews of his or her work all tend to polish the ability of a historian to produce magisterial books and articles. A senior historian is identified as an authority in a particular field for a reason, one that has been constantly tested over a long career. Professors like to see their books in students' bibliographies.

That said, it is important to ask whether this great, established authority is writing in the same sub-discipline of history in which that reputation was established. If, say, an eminent historian of ancient Greece writes a book on ancient China, does his or her reputation reinforce or reduce the authority of that text? Can the knowledge base and methodology of one area of history be transferred to any other without losing some measure of gravity? I think the answer is unclear. First, ask why the classical European historian is writing on Asia to begin with and then judge whether the evidence and the research is appropriate for his or her conclusions. Does he or she read Chinese? Was there original research done in the archives or with original documents? Is the weight of received scholarship in the field duly acknowledged and applied? Often, changing fields, like any change in perspective, can bring new light on well-established areas of research; intellectual cross-pollination is good. But if the result is a superficial study, based on printed secondary work in translation, it is reasonable to question the authority of the work.

Also, older historians were trained in the latest methods in use during the early years of their careers. Most successful scholars develop with their disciplines, learning new techniques and methods as they emerge from the academy. Historians, despite what they do, are hardly frozen in time; indeed, more so than most scholars they recognize the need to change with the study of their discipline. So, it would be unjust and foolish not to use the recent work of an older scholar, because it is in these that you will often find the most subtle and profound insights.

However, knowledge in history, as in every discipline, is developing so quickly it would be impossible for any historian, old or young, to master all of the methods and tools now available. And, new perspectives and sub-disciplines are emerging that need to be taken into account to provide a broader and richer picture of the past. For example, Gender History and Queer History have illuminated previously unspoken or understudied areas of the past. Big History has developed to put human civilization into the context of the development of the planet and the universe; and Environmental History has trained historians' sights on climate and its relationship to human civilization. Food History makes the connection between agriculture, nutrition, and historical change. There are a great many more examples of recent new methods of historical study, But, how is a student to use them all or find which perspectives are most useful to a given assignment in a specific course? The answer is to follow the thread of evidence revealed in the core texts in your area of interest. A professional historian in writing a book for publication will have taken most of these new perspectives into account as necessary.

So, the age of the historian is not an important element in deciding which historians to use for your research. But, the age of the book and hence the research are very important considerations. Generally speaking, the more recent the book or article the more current and hence effective the research and analysis. Recent scholarship builds on the work of others that came before and that includes the kinds of new methods and tools I mentioned above. New discoveries of documents and sources are always being made; and there is a constant review of received knowledge within university history departments which require us to re-evaluate and refine our work. Don't look at the age of the historian, then; look at the date of the book! And, if you find several editions of the same book, use the most recent, as earlier misconceptions, mistakes, or infelicities should have been caught and excised.

History by Non-Historians

Finally, what can we say about history written by non-historians? There are many categories into which these studies fall, some of them obvious, some less so. For example, if a journalist chooses to research and write an account of a historical event or period which he or she saw and chronicled for newspapers and magazines, does the author automatically become a historian? To some extent, yes, as the immediate evidence collected for the newspaper articles also constitute the stuff of history. And, there is obvious skill in analysis, as is putting the event into a wider context. But, what should we think about a journalist writing about medieval France? Are perhaps the very strengths and experience that brought some authority to a study of current events be detrimental to an understanding of a society very different and long past, one that requires completely different skills, knowledge, and research? Often, although not always, the popular or contemporary writer fails when confronting the past. It is far too distant a country with customs and practices far too different to generate the quick observations and telling quotations that gave such immediacy to an article in a magazine.

That is not to say that journalists who record their experience as history cannot produce great work. It is a historian's joke that the difference between a journalist and a historian is 50 years. There is truth to that because the immediacy of newspaper reporting must be sacrificed to the considered analysis, careful study, and thoughtful reflection required of more profound works of history. So, again, it is useful to know the direction from which a historian approaches his or her subject but it is unwise to reject a work as necessarily superficial or popular merely because the author was not fully trained as a historian. Nevertheless, some evidence of an appropriate level of understanding, skill, and insight should be seen: anyone – for example, a crossing guard in the street – can describe an event experienced firsthand; but that record becomes only one element of what must be a wider and more complete study because the crossing guard did not know what to look for, how to broaden the experience into a useful reflection of the importance of the event, and likely lacked the training to make the description clear and vibrant. His observation constituted part of the evidence, then, but would likely not be sufficient in itself.

This leads to that question of style and authority. My students have so often complained that my commentary on their essays seemed to concentrate more on how they structured their papers and their diction than on the content of the work. And, they are quite right. Style functions in many ways in the creation of history. We have already noted the classical and humanist perspective that history was a branch of rhetoric and a grand style was needed to carry the reader along, convince him or her of the validity of one's conclusions, and provide uplifting examples, brilliantly drawn, that could rise to become almost a moral force. For history to be useful and vital, they believed, it had to be powerfully written and completely engaging.

There is a small element of value in this: it is in fact easier to understand something well written and clearly formulated than something constructed with faulty syntax and language. It is also more memorable, as our classically trained historians believed; and it is more pleasant to read, especially for longer periods of time. But what we need to emphasize here is clarity and effect, not merely elegance and style. Style is a tool not an end in our modern academic historian's world. Precision in language and a logical architecture need to vitalize the historian's craft; but these are equally dependent on the evidence provided and the strength of the conclusions drawn. History is not poetry, nor is it a stream of consciousness free association of ideas. The style must reflect the conventions of expository prose and the greatest compliment any reader can deliver is that the book is clearly written and well organized.

So, pay attention to style and put the style in the context of the author's biography. A work written in the seventeenth or eighteenth centuries will have a very different vocabulary and style. Sentences will be longer and the meaning of words sometimes elusive. Again, these are not reasons to reject the historian but another opportunity to understand the conventions under which he was writing: it offers another insight into the age that created the work and the mind of the author.

Historical Jargon

Another element of style that has become ever more burdensome is the development of new vocabularies and constructions, really jargon. These emerged not so much as a general trend across all historical writing as identifiers for specific sub-genres of history. Thus, you will discover that social historians, for example, have one set of vocabularies and stylistic assumptions and economic historians another. Indeed, every sub-category of historian has developed such instruments and these consequently provide a form of secret handshake in their communities and operate under the assumption that only their own kind will read their work; or, if you wish to enter their court, you had better know what to say and how to say it. In fact, such uses of jargon or even formulaic structures among professional historians can be exclusionary to the uninitiated general reader and reflect that modern movement away from history as rhetoric – or even as history as a subject in the humanities – to history as an ideological tool or a form of social science that merits its own terminology, like any other science or quasi science.

To a very large degree, this is inescapable. It is a function of the narrowing of all intellectual disciplines and the fragmentation of knowledge. So, what is to be done? There is no turning back, except to rely on more 'popular' historians or generalists whose synoptic interpretations are directed precisely towards a wide readership and general audience. A student or scholar, however, cannot rely solely on such work; they need the research, knowledge, and insights of a specialist. Consequently, the only solution is to approach works heavily laden with jargon and specialized code words as a kind of foreign language. Learn what the jargon means and how the code can be applied to reveal the content. It is never very difficult because the range of such terms and codes tends to be small; still, it is important to cross that barrier to mine what material is hidden in the code and to understand how the evidence is interpreted and used so that you can draw legitimate conclusions.

History in Translation

If jargon or a disciplinary secret language is at work in English, to what extent can a student completely trust a work of history that is read only in translation? The original was devised in a different language and language is a reflection of deeply understood allusions, cultural references, and intellectual traditions. Again, there is nothing else we can really do but trust that the translator has understood the original and rendered it in English in a clear and honest manner. And, of course, we cannot really determine the validity of our trust in the translation: if we had that depth of knowledge we would have read the book or article in the original.

One of the few ways to get a handle on a translation, though, is to read the translator's introduction or preface, if there is one attached to the book. Often these will describe the principles which the translator followed or reflect on the difficulties encountered in the original text. In general, in fact, rather than simply ignoring these kinds of front matter in books, it is very useful to read them carefully, because you will have a defined 'advance organizer' (to use a bit of jargon) which can help in the interpretation and assessment of a work of history.

So, let's conclude by rehearsing what has been said in this chapter. In effect, I am saying that the historian is just as important as the history – occasionally even more so. To get the full advantage out of any text, it is imperative that you assess who wrote it, when it was written, and for whom. The perspective and conditioning of the author will determine to a large degree what form the analysis will take and what kinds of conclusions will be drawn. And, looking carefully and deeply at the circumstances of the historian will also help in understanding the history itself because he or she is inscribing a record both of the area of history covered in the book and the time in which the historian lived. Historiography is a wonderful way to access the past as we can follow the intellectual and cultural assumptions of the historian. Consequently, investigating the historian can offer a double reward. On the one hand we have the value of the material in the work itself, the research and the analysis and conclusions; and, we have an insight into the intellectual environment of the author, giving us an understanding of his or her world as well.

The old, nineteenth-century dictum of the great German historian, Leopold von Ranke (*d.* 1886), that a historian should just 'tell is like it was' is neat but impossible. The historian must be more than an empirical observer, a recorder, and arranger of evidence. What is more useful is to join the telling with the story told so our appreciation of the past can become deep and complex. The pasts that made us are a guide to who we are but en route we can engage in conversation with many of those who have taken us there, the historians and chroniclers of the past who defined our sense of self by filtering received knowledge through their experience. History is, remember, the study of people written by other people.

3

If not the Historian, then Certainly the Evidence

The Nature of Evidence

If we can't trust historians as being always the reliable narrators of events and unbiased recorders of the past, can we at least trust the documents and other forms of evidence that survive from earlier times as having an inherent legitimacy and unvarnished authority, free from the kinds of considerations needed to assess the writers of history, as we discussed in the previous chapter? In other words, if we take the interpreter of evidence out of the process of recording history, would we have a clearer and more accurate insight into the past?

The short answer is, of course, no. The explanation derives from the same considerations that drove our need to assess the role of the historian: the evidence of earlier times was written by people who, like historians, had particular purposes and perspectives that cannot help but be reflected in what they write. Even the most transactional evidence of the past must be evaluated to test its validity. Material such as legal documents, mercantile contracts, eye-witness descriptions – including drawings and photographs – statutes, and political minutes or debates all result from the intervention of men and women who produced them, organized them, conserved them, and perhaps interpreted them.

This is a difficult concept for students in particular to accept. When faced with a collection of primary source documents, each appearing

The Experience of History, First Edition. Kenneth Bartlett.

to state a 'fact' about a certain aspect of the past, the general response is to see it as 'fact', a true statement of the circumstances or situation described. That nineteenth-century dictum of von Ranke of 'telling it like was' derived heavily from his collection of evidence, presenting it and then acknowledging that information's source in clear footnotes so that it appeared that there was complete transparency. It was an important development in the writing of history and one which remains central to the profession we practise as historians today. Every student and scholar must reveal his or her sources; and these must be allowed to speak as memories collected from those whose experience was closer to the events under scrutiny.

The act of separating primary sources – documents written in the period under investigation – from secondary sources – a later analysis or narrative of events – also introduces the observation that what a historian wrote is greater than the sum of his or her evidence: the process of organizing, interpreting, and weighing the evidence constitutes a contribution to our understanding of the past that will in itself offer deeper understanding and add to the received historiography on the subject. In reading the historian's assessment of the evidence, we know we must consider his or her level of objectivity; but equally we must ask about how the very choice of documents used as historical evidence conditioned the results. Given the large gaps in our knowledge and in the evidence, and given the forces at work on the historian using this material, can any evidence – primary or secondary – really be truly objective? A document might perhaps be considered objective but its use will be the conscious intervention of the historian; hence that very distinction between primary and secondary source blurs, and qualifies the idea that anyone at any time can in fact 'tell it like it was'.

The later nineteenth century hardly introduced such rigorous mechanisms for the acknowledgement of evidence. Classical historians, such as Tacitus (Publius Cornelius Tacitus, *c.* 56–*c.* 117 AD), used documentary proof for the validity of their narratives. And, in the fifteenth century Leonardo Bruni (*d.* 1444) in his *History of the Florentine People* used primary documents as well as older histories and chronicles; he then weighed their respective value in reaching what he believed to be true conclusions about past events. He was followed in the next century by his fellow Florentine Francesco Guicciardini (1483–1540) who when compiling his *History of Italy* even carried official documents to his palace and villa in Florence to ensure that he got it right. A great number of other examples could be found to show that historians in earlier times were very concerned about evidence and how to employ it, even though the results are not entirely what a modern professional historian would expect. These writers were reacting to the acceptance of the kinds of sources which previous writers had uncritically accepted as useful evidence, including such things as legends, fables, anecdotal observations, and even chronicles that recorded everything the author thought significant or merely interesting, whether true – or even possible – or not.

But, all of these historians made choices as to what evidence they would use and how it would be interpreted. Evidence in itself is a tool, the raw material of historical writing, not absolute truth that somehow supersedes the operation of human frailty. Historians do not merely arrange and then draw conclusions from recorded truth: they add but another layer of intervention between the past and their readers.

So, how can historians at any time assess the validity of the evidence they use? The first point of engagement is to always ask who wrote the document, for what purpose, for what audience and when. Let me give you some examples.

Taxation Records

Taxation records survive for almost every society for which there are extant written documents. It was in everyone's interest to conserve such materials in order to provide evidence in case of dispute, to forecast future revenues, or as protection for the taxpayer or tax collector. Many societies required – and still require – self-assessment and reporting, that is, trusting the taxpayer to report all appropriate income, property, expenses, and deductions. Most modern countries use this form of self-assessment and there are many examples in more distant history, such as the Florentine *catasto* of 1427. But, you need to ask, what was the strongest motivation in calculating income and net worth in the process of self-assessment? Obviously, it was to minimize taxable income and wealth to pay the lowest tax possible and keep more for yourself. Provided that the regulations governing legitimate deductions were transparently applied, this method should be a very reliable guide to an individual's or a family's real economic position because the penalties for false statements are always severe. However, can we in fact trust that taxpayers accurately reflected their situation? In many cases income or property is not declared or wealth is hidden. Similarly, wealth is often transferred to other family members, to companies, or even other jurisdictions. Without having a complete portfolio of taxation records in which an individual or family appears, a historian would always have to assume that wealth is legally or illegally under-reported.

Conversely, what about those societies which required fiscal officials to assess an individual's tax, based on a survey of his or her property, income, lifestyle, and other indicators of economic position? Well, the opposite situation from the example above of self-assessment obtains. It is in the official's and the state's best interest to maximize wealth to gain the largest tax assessment possible. This is particularly true in those societies, such as *ancien régime* France, which relied on tax farmers, those companies or consortia which purchased the right from the Crown to collect taxes in a particular locality. In this system, a kind of auction resulted in the highest bidder winning the right to collect royal taxation and usually paid that amount up front. The profit resulted from the spread between what the tax farmer initially paid and what his officials managed to squeeze from that tax district. In such instances it is almost always wise to assume that assessments are at the highest possible level, sometimes constrained by law, sometimes not.

What the above examples of taxation records should indicate is that evidence which on the surface appears to be among the most reliable and objective possible is really driven by whoever compiled the records, by how the law was interpreted, by how rigorously the institutions of the state operated or the compliance of the individual determined. In other words, all evidence must be evaluated according to its context and tested by other information to decide its degree of validity. To make the kinds of judgments necessary to determine how wealthy someone in the past really was, the historian needs to know a great deal more than just what his or her tax records declared. The historian must understand how taxes were collected, the culture of compliance or non-compliance, the penalties imposed for false declarations and the rate of prosecution and conviction, and whether there might be additional financial evidence not included in the taxation records. Consequently, it must be stressed that any single source of evidence will inevitably be less useful and valid; everything must be evaluated in the context of other records which reinforce or challenge the burden of that evidence.

Court or Legal Documents

Another example: what about court documents, that is, evidence of legal prosecution, trials and convictions or exonerations? Once more, on the surface, this evidence should be among the most reliable, as it was in the interest of the state, the law itself, and all involved in the process of justice that the evidence be correct and complete. Again, however, think about the nature of evidence in an adversarial legal system. The prosecution will collect as much evidence as possible, including personal testimony, which will prove the accused guilty. The defence will, naturally, do the same to prove innocence. In those few examples where the evidence exhibited and the briefs for both the prosecution and defence survive, the historian can draw reasonable conclusions about whether the judgment against the accused was just or not and extrapolate accordingly. But, when dealing with the records of the past, how often does such complete evidence survive? And, if you have only part of the evidence and testimony, which position is most fully represented? And, can we be sure that witnesses or prosecutors were telling the truth without some degree of independent verification?

Furthermore, the historian must understand how the legal and court system which produced the evidence worked at the time the documents were produced. To what extent could the accused have access to the evidence of the prosecution? Did the courts function independently of those in power in the state or society? Could the accused offer a defence at all? These kinds of considerations reflected the nature of the documentation that was produced and to a degree survives. Once again, then, the context of the evidence is as important as the evidence itself, if a historian intends to make a fair judgment about an event in the past. Having a record, even a relatively complete record, is really not enough: that record must be interpreted through the lens of the society that produced it.

Think about some very basic questions when dealing with evidence, especially legal documents. Who was on trial for what? Who were his or her accusers? Who constituted the judge, judicial panel, jury, court officials, lawyers, and who kept public order? Did rich people who were literate and enjoyed influence and powerful connections receive a different – and perhaps more sympathetic – hearing than a poor, illiterate prisoner from another place? To what degree did society, or the state, have a stake in a conviction? Was torture or its threat used, and can you accept evidence, even a signed confession, obtained by torture?

The farther we go into the past the more difficult these issues become. In part, this is because of the imperfect survival of records. But, the passage of time also takes us into that very different country which is the past. There our assumptions about how institutions worked and people behaved no longer operate with clarity or complete comprehension. In most instances we do know what the law was, as laws were recorded with great solemnity; but we don't know how those laws were interpreted or enforced, unless the context of the usual practices of the society is understood. For example, to declare, when drunk, in a public place that the king is a fool and his dynasty will end with his death could, depending on the jurisdiction, be a capital offence and lead to execution, or, it could be a misdemeanour, perhaps prosecuted as drunk, disorderly conduct, or it could be no crime at all, merely idle talk. What matters, then, is the context and jurisdiction, as well as the law and the nature of the alleged offence. If the kingdom were at risk, such as struggling in a civil war, the law could certainly be applied more harshly because the stakes were greater. Again, the historian needs to put the evidence and the record in a wider perspective and test it with other evidence to judge its validity and immediate significance.

Eye-Witness Evidence

If apparently official, well-kept, and scrupulous recorded evidence, such as tax or legal records, must be carefully tested to judge its validity, what about other kinds of evidence, especially those survivals from the past that seem again to offer some reliable information? This category of evidence consists of testimony such as first-person accounts, written by someone involved in or witnessing an event under investigation. These sorts of documents have great value if used carefully, but I remind you of our discussion of historians writing history in the previous chapter. What did the writer have to gain or lose? Whose side was he or she on? How close was the observer really to the event witnessed? Was the writer actually there, as attested, or was his or her presence a literary or rhetorical effect to give the text greater authority? Who was with the writer, and why was he or she there at all?

First-person evidence, recorded either for posterity or for personal use, is a wonderful resource to capture the flavour of the past; and often these kinds of reports are all we have of private events or moments when the official record is silent. But, be careful. The evidence is in effect a piece of singular history largely dependent on one person's perception; and we all know how perceptions can be influenced by other considerations and consequently are unreliable.

For instance, take the example of the kind of event that occurs with some regularity today. You failed to return home one night, arriving only at 6:00 a.m. to find your father or mother (or any other character with a deep interest in your whereabouts) sitting waiting for you. You are required to explain why you were so late and so you do, hopefully to their satisfaction. Once in your room, however, you telephone your best friend and describe the events of that night in exquisite detail. But, your friend had already heard from the person you were with and received a quite different description of the night's adventure. So, which version is 'true'? All have an eye witness who not only saw the events of that night but who was a central character in whatever drama unfolded; you, the eye witness, delivered two probably mutually exclusive accounts, and if investigated, those events could very likely be interpreted in yet another way by another observer, as they were by your friend's earlier caller. Your story to your parents probably amounts to telling them what they wanted to hear or what put your actions in the best light. Your testimony to your friend probably exaggerated your experience, made you a more significant or interesting participant in the night's drama. And, you know in your conscience that both of your accounts were elaborated; and that third party witness had described that night in a very different way. This is the problem with personal evidence and even official documentation based on personal evidence. The validity of it depends on the audience and the circumstances of the principal actors. This is the problem you face as a historian confronting apparently reliable but inconsistent evidence.

Using Evidence Requires Skill and Experience

Finally, in assessing written records, especially older documents, it is important to have the skills to read and interpret them critically, in ways not altogether necessary for modern records. If the documents are written by hand, you must be confident that you can decipher every letter, especially irregular words like proper names. If the original record dates from almost any time before approximately the seventeenth century, you will need to be familiar with abbreviations commonly used, as these can change the meaning of words significantly. You need to have experience with formulaic phrases, standard usage, and most importantly dating and authentication, like seals or notarial marks or witnesses' signatures. Very often these things are clues to the validity of the record itself: forgers or interpolators make mistakes in legal formulas, syntax, vocabulary, or usage. Styles of handwriting, the means of dating, signing, sealing, and even folding documents can be clues about who wrote and prepared the document, when it was written and where. In the European Middle Ages and Renaissance especially references to currency, units of measurement, distance, or even time were highly local, and these things are important clues. But, again, handle such things with great care.

For example, if you have a record that asks for payment in Venetian ducats or Florentine florins, it would be reasonable to assume that the documents were prepared for a Venetian or Florentine or sent to one of those citizens or written in Venice or Florence. Again, this seems reasonable; but it is not necessarily the case at all. Because early local European coinage was notoriously unreliable, fluctuating greatly depending on such factors as the silver content, international transactions were often recorded in the stable gold coinage of those two Italian cities. It would be a serious mistake to attribute the content of the document to them. Usually, there is an indication of the place the record was made at the end of the document, in the 'dated at' conclusion. The names of any notary that recorded the document can also provide evidence of where the evidence was written; and very often internal evidence within the document can reveal this information. So, again, we must be very assiduous in unpacking the many kinds of evidence contained in a single early record. Reading such documents requires knowledge, skill, experience, and insight. Documentary evidence is therefore a mine of information and each document can provide a great many bits of knowledge of the past. But they are equally a minefield and require careful use. Documentary evidence, then, is never absolutely reliable in itself; and once again there will be a layer of intervention by the historian, interpreting and making sense of a record written long ago and which today necessitates interpretation for it to be useful in investigating the past.

Drawings as Evidence

In my discussion of first-person evidence, I specifically referred to records preserved in writing. What about visual records, such as drawings, paintings or even photographs? Surely, this is an incontrovertible record of an event captured either by a trained eye and skilled hand or a machine that faithfully reproduced what the lens saw. But, again, is it? In the example of a drawing, one must ask the degree of artistic licence used. Artists are exactly that: artists. The intent might certainly be to describe something as accurately as possible; but artists are trained and almost reflexively use principles of design and interpretation to ensure that the drawing or painting is a work of art as well as an image of what the artist saw. Often additional figures are added for complexity and drama; or the interaction and distribution of the figures might be altered to give the work more a more fluid, interesting or arresting effect. Costumes might be changed to allow for decorum or elicit pity or anger; facial expressions can be caught to illustrate the artist's own feelings about the event. And, I could go on; but the point should be clear. Drawings and especially paintings, include other imperatives than simply 'telling it like it was' visually. To be sure, these are very important documents, produced by an eye-witness trained to observe carefully. But they are also more than mere documentary evidence: they are works of art, hence at least in part works of the imagination and equally subject to interpretation.

So, again, the visual record must be tested by comparing it to other evidence. Complex questions must be asked that will usually result in further research: was the artist in reality there or did he or she rely on the descriptions of witnesses? Was the drawing done at the site or later in a studio from rough sketches? Why was the drawing made? Who was the artist and how did that artist participate in the event? Drawings, then, are no more 'true' than written observations, and indeed require another level of assessment because of their genre. And they very often require another skill set, as interpreting images is not at all the same as interpreting written records. Think of the role of the court artist today in those jurisdictions where cameras are not permitted during a trial. What expression did the artist choose to capture? Was the accused drawn in a way to move us to pity, to make him or her sympathetic or terrifyingly ugly and thus capable of committing a terrible crime? Did the nature of the alleged crime drive how the accused was portrayed? Was the subject drawn as 'looking guilty'? Again, the need for more information is required in order to test visual records.

Photographs as Evidence

But surely photographs are absolutely reliable because the camera is a machine that captures an image of what was there! This would result, then, in a reasonable acceptance of photographs as unassailable evidence; but, again, a camera is a machine operated by a person, and the photo can be altered or taken to serve a particular purpose.

Modern cameras capture a moment in that fraction of a second when the shutter is opened. So, what is recorded is that exact moment, not what led to it or what followed. Unless the image has been tampered with (always a consideration that must be investigated), the picture is extremely useful in placing a person at the scene of an event – but not why he or she was there, for example. Photographs put innocent bystanders in the action of violent demonstrations, or at the scene of a crime that the person in the picture might not have been aware was committed. A raised hand or a particular expression could look culpable, although these gestures could be completely innocent and simply an accident of when the photo was taken. So, again look at the circumstantial evidence in the photograph. Is the dress of the person appropriate for what the picture records? Look closely at facial expression and the reaction of other people around him or her. Who took the photograph and why? Is it part of a series or a unique example? Can you see any corroborating detail to place the photograph in place and time, such as street names, the time of day or year, advertisements or visible documents, such as posters or magazines that can testify to the date? In other words, you, as a historian, need to investigate photographic evidence with exactly the same degree of rigour that you applied to written records and documents. And, like written records, the actual photograph becomes a piece of evidence in itself, helping validate the content so that you are able to make a reasonable and confident judgment as to its accuracy and reliability.

Aural Evidence

Many of the same considerations above must be applied to aural records, that is, evidence recorded as sound. Although a tape of someone's testimony, conversation, or inflammatory speech can have a powerful ring of truth, this evidence is as slippery as written or visual documents. First, ask the same questions of any piece of evidence: who recorded the tape, where, when, why, and for whom. Add to this whether those present were aware they were being recorded. Is this a tape from a wiretap or a hidden recording device; or does it result from an open conversation? And, as with so many written records, experience and skill are needed to fill in gaps, make reasonable conjectures about muffled or indistinct words, identify who among several interlocutors is speaking, and whether references to earlier, unrecorded conversations are important to understand the full implication and meaning of the tape.

One very famous example should illustrate why taped evidence is as tricky as any other kind of documentary material. Between 1971 and 1973 US President Richard Nixon recorded over 10,000 hours of taped conversation in the Oval Office, Cabinet Room, and later several other locations; telephones were also tapped. Some of those taped knew about the recording protocol; others did not. The recorder was voice activated, so in theory nothing said would be lost. Therefore, given the volume of information and the comprehensive nature of the recordings, a very rich and authoritative archive of material should be available on those tapes. And, this is true: the tapes are a remarkable cache of historical evidence, an almost unique insight into an American president's words and actions. Nevertheless, because there were obviously a great many conversations not recorded or important material transmitted on paper, it is still necessary to corroborate much of the information through other sources; and care must be taken when drawing conclusions, given that some of those involved were aware they were being taped and others not.

Furthermore, the comprehensive nature of the tapes was seriously compromised by the infamous 18½ minute gap, caused, as she confessed, by Nixon's secretary. Although the confession of the secretary was implausible and although we know from other sources the important subject of the probably culpable discussion that filled those lost minutes, the evidence is gone forever. The content of that gap was been the subject of over 40 years of speculation by historians, as has the question of who really erased the tapes and why.

I use this example because it has become the most celebrated instance of the importance of aural evidence. It is also, despite its very professional operation and archiving, a perfect example of why such evidence needs both corroboration and skilful use. If documents intended for archival purposes using the latest technology and operated by the most professional sound technicians reporting to one of the most powerful men in the world can have mysterious gaps and some muffled words or ambiguous references, what about simple wiretaps or recordings made for other purposes? Once again, my advice is to apply carefully all the lessons of historical research to such material: find corroboration in other documents if possible, identify who knew what when and why the recordings were made, and in whose interest it would be either to erase or preserve such material. Modern evidence produced by modern technology requires the same care as a medieval manuscript.

Missing or Negative Evidence

Missing evidence is the huge volume of records that did not survive or that was never recorded at all. This absence of documentation can equally be constructed positively as negative evidence because, although this material provides no definitive information, it can be interpreted to deliver extremely important insights, such as why some expected records were not kept or no longer survive. Odd as it may appear, negative evidence can be extremely useful in drawing conclusions about the past. In essence, this form of evidence operates in two different ways. First, there are the silences in a historical record, that is, what surviving documents do NOT say. Second, there are those individual records, series, or entire archives that have disappeared, despite clear indications that they once existed. Can these lost or silent documents still be of use and tell us something about the past? Let's look first at the silences, lacunae, or missing material within records.

Every historian has a large store of personal experience concerning missing evidence: usually it is a story of a fruitless search or a frustrating anomaly. Sometimes, the missing documentation is as simple as a name not recorded, making what could otherwise have been a very useful bit of evidence useless; sometimes it is a missing piece of correspondence which would explain the puzzling and tantalizing reference in a subsequent letter; sometimes it is a block of missing documents that interrupt a series, resulting in a serious loss of authority for those documents that remain. The list could be expanded greatly, as preserving evidence was not usually as important in the past as it is today. But, what we must recognize is that the very absence of documents is often an important clue. For example, if a great many letters from an individual are lost from a rich exchange of correspondence, can we assume that those letters were consciously removed by someone for a particular purpose, usually relating to their content? This is a very reasonable conclusion and could tell a researcher a great deal about someone's attitude to the author or recipient of those letters, the values of society at the time, the position of the correspondents and their relationship, or the subsequent attempt by others to alter the evidence to ensure that proof of something could not be found. Again, the possibilities are vast; but a historian working in a particular area can often follow his or her experience, deep knowledge of the circumstances and the individuals involved to draw some effective conclusions. So, again, the evidence is imperfect and much depends on the intervention, imagination, knowledge, and intentions of the historian; and, as a result, some dark places in the past might receive some light.

Even in official records, lacunae can mean a great deal. Why would someone remove a series of legal, fiscal, or administrative documents, for example? Again, the motives are as numerous as the varieties of human fears and ambitions. But, there could be evidence of malfeasance in office, or evidence used in another context, like a trial, that required that they be collected and stored elsewhere; it is even possible as in the case of Guicciardini (*d.* 1540) or later Samuel Pepys (1633–1703) that these documents were employed by writers or historians in the past for reasons altogether different from the purposes for which they were written, such as subsequent historical research. Once more, an experienced modern historian will investigate why there are breaks in series of records; and deep familiarity with the period and the people involved can often lead to plausible conjecture. The evidence might well be imperfect but not altogether silent, as it often leaves a shadow or a memory.

Similarly, a missing document can reveal a great deal about a moment in the past, although perhaps not the information you were looking for. Let me give you an example from my own research. Many years ago I was tracing a group of foreign students who were studying at Italian universities in the late sixteenth century, some taking degrees, some not. I had a significant collection of documents from letters, university records, and reports from authorities about their behaviour, and even some material on where and with whom they lived. I traced one individual to the University of Ferrara where he was known to have taken a degree, a doctoral degree, a relatively rare and distinguished achievement that usually generates various records.

I went to Ferrara, followed the complex trail of where evidence of his degree might be found; and because degrees were granted on the authority of the archbishop I had to search the archiepiscopal records but found no evidence of his doctorate, something I was desperate to uncover because of the rich evidence found in such a document, such as the names of his fellow students who witnessed his degree, the identities of his examiners and what, exactly, he was examined on. But, there was no record in the repository where it should have been preserved.

At that point, I learnt that students for advanced degrees at that time almost all used the same notary in Ferrara to make a copy of the document; and that was especially true of foreigners. I sought out the notarial records, which were housed in a completely different archive, and requested the notarial volume for the appropriate year. I then went page by page through the *notarile*. I found a great many foreign doctorates recorded for that year; and then I found a page headed by the name of the man I was searching for, giving the date on which the degree was granted – but the page and the one following were blank!

The notary had indeed been engaged to record the degree; and he was anticipating the work to the point that he inserted a page in a bound folio and inscribed it with the student's name; but the doctorate was never transcribed. The reason for this was that the notary had to be paid a not insubstantial sum for this record; and rather than pay the fee the student left town without ever having his degree recorded. He chose to save the money over having a permanent notarial record of his doctorate.

This discovery taught me a great deal about the man I was researching. It confirmed my impression that he was something of a rogue, and that he had constant financial problems and that he had no intention of remaining in Italy, which would have made the documentation of his degree more useful. He had no family close by and was likely not close to his fellow students who would have witnessed for him; and he could not have cared at all whether the names of his distinguished examiners were known. So, in many ways I found nothing in that document; but I learnt a great deal from the negative evidence.

I provide this example because it illustrates once more that evidence is not what students often think it is. Even when records survive in substantial amounts they need interpretation; but in this case the failure to survive constitutes important evidence as well. Because all evidence must be interpreted by the historian, we need to recognize that lack of documentation needs to be investigated and the insights applied to your research. So, failure to find something does in fact constitute a kind of evidence nonetheless. Can we trust these inferences? That is a decision you, as a historian, must make. Again, there is no such thing as 'pure' truth in historical records, except for the most basic elements, and even these need to be validated. Once again, evidence is the working capital of historians and it is they who make the preserved and silent records speak.

The loss of entire archives or series of records needs to be addressed as well because these depravations have truly affected our ability to interpret the past. The world is a dangerous place for records, as well as for people. The regular visitations of fire, flood, war, and simple neglect have resulted in the loss of untold millions of documents. These documentary catastrophes have made our knowledge of the past incomplete and again forces historians to use their imaginations and experience and other surviving clues to put the pieces back together as far as possible. In some cases this is very difficult, if not impossible, and we are occasionally left with a singular source for very important periods in human history. To what extent can we verify all of the statements of ancient historians, such as Livy, Tacitus, or that most salacious of descriptions of the personal activities of the first 12 Roman emperors found in Suetonius (*The Lives of the Twelve Caesars* by Gaius Suetonius Tranquillus, *c.* 69 – after 122 AD)? There is very little evidence to apply as a control for their observations; so historians of ancient Rome need to be careful in accepting all of their assertions as true, even if those writers are the only evidence that survives. Very often other writers and books are mentioned; but these fail to survive, so to what extent do later historians simply accept the assertion that there is corroboration or sources for important conclusions when the evidence can't be read and assessed? So, as indicated above, we work with what we have to try to fill in the gaps wherever we can. But, once more we need to assert that evidence is not the absolute record we would like.

Similarly, there are examples of entire archives either lost or destroyed in part because of conscious political, military, or personal decisions. There is a general belief, for example, that the first emperor of China, Qin Shi Huangdi (260–210 BC), after uniting the country, took the advice of his chancellor and ordered all of the books of history and Confucian thought up to 213 BC destroyed; and he ordered the execution of the most important 460 scholars who kept alive this tradition. In this way, history would begin with the Qin dynasty; and its first emperor would be seen as the beginning of a new age where there could be no subversive opposition to his rule and no hostile evidence about the years before his reign. Although modern research has softened this ancient story somewhat, there was a great burning of books and the two copies of each which were to be kept in the emperor's collection were all subsequently lost to posterity. Evidence, then, was destroyed in the most systematic way, and such acts make it difficult to develop rich interpretations of past events.

In the ancient west, a similar practice of ***damnatio memoriae*** attempted to strike from history the memory, in fact the very name, of people who were seen as hostile. Inscriptions were struck out, coins melted down, and names removed from official records. This attempt was hardly ever completely successful, but it signifies another warning to the historian that the surviving evidence might not be complete or might have been severely tampered with in order to influence how the past would be remembered. More recently, in Germany, the Nazis in the 1930s had ritual burnings of books they deemed decadent, hostile, or written by those they sought to silence completely.

One of Europe's greatest losses of records resulted from the megalomania of Napoleon Bonaparte (1769–1821). Napoleon wanted Paris to be the centre of Europe, and one of his plans was to create a huge Archive of the Empire from the National Archives begun modestly for French material by the Revolutionary government. Documents from across Italy and elsewhere were requisitioned; but in particular Napoleon wanted material from the Vatican Archives. Books, manuscripts, and records, as well as art objects, were to be collected and sent to Paris. Between 1810 and 1813, well over 3,000 wooden crates of documents from the entire history of the church were set to France. Some were lost or damaged en route but the vast majority arrived safely. The fall of Napoleon in 1814 resulted in the decision to return all such material to Rome; but neither the restored French Bourbon king, Louis XVIII, nor the pope wanted to pay the vast amount necessary for the packing and returning of the documents. To save expense while generating cash, thousands of documents from the Middle Ages and after were sold as scrap paper: over 800 fewer crates of documents returned to Rome. Some of the important manuscripts sold were bought – or stolen – by collectors, so we know where they now are; and some have later been returned or donated to various repositories, including those relating to the trial of Galileo which were given back to Rome in the mid-nineteenth century. But, many thousands of important records were lost forever. Consequently, for those researching the history of the Church or papacy or any number of important legal cases that came before church law, the gaps in the records are infuriating, especially because they need not have disappeared. However, knowing this, and understanding the restrictions imposed by the loss helps both explicate how even the best archives of documents are fragile in a dangerous world and how the historian is always confined by what remains. That intuition and experience I mentioned before are therefore not as useful in such circumstances in making sense of a past left imperfectly documented by incomplete records, because the loss is often random, with some evidence surviving and other documents lost. Certainly, the better you know an archive the better your intuition will be regarding what was lost, its importance and even its content; but sometimes intuition is not enough.

Conclusion

In conclusion, then, I am arguing that there is no such thing as absolutely unambiguous or incontrovertible evidence. Evidence is the working material of historians who interpret and apply it to craft their conclusions about events in the past. But the evidence, like the histories written from it, was the work of people who had their own motives and failings. There are no 'facts' except those agreed pegs, like dates, on which we historians hang our analysis. The evidence constitutes an interpretation of events just as much as history written from that evidence is an interpretation of events. We are consequently always at several removes from the lives of those now long gone. They are not altogether forgotten, as they have left their marks in the evidence that survives. It is for us, as historians, to interpret those accidental survivals and make sense of them, being honest and fair in our judgments, although constrained by the evidence itself and our ability to fully understand its significance or even meaning, separated as we are by time and familiarity of the experience of the past.

4

The Periods and Divisions of History

In the previous chapter we investigated what kinds of evidence survive and how they should be used, with particular concern for the problems that all material from the past carries with it and how these might be addressed. But evidence is the raw material of historical investigation. What we need to discuss now are the divisions and temporal categories of historical writing and how best to determine the most effective approach to understanding the past and how best to organize evidence in a coherent manner to draw convincing conclusions. The major and most traditional categories into which the past is divided are chronological and geographical: these tend to be the elemental organizing principles behind any work of historical research. Let's begin with periodization, as this is among the most contentious elements of historical analysis and one which requires much thought and explication.

Historical Periodization: History as Chunks of Time

When temporal periods, such as the Ancient World, the Middle Ages, the Renaissance, the Age of Exploration, or even simply the nineteenth century, inform the titles of history books, readers and students generally recognize the years being investigated and can pursue their research accordingly. This is obviously a convenient way to organize the vast repository of information about the past and one that has been used

The Experience of History, First Edition. Kenneth Bartlett.

almost from the beginning of historical writing. However, as in most things historical, there are disagreements as to what should constitute a coherent period in the past. There are no fixed beginnings or ends in historiography, only convenient chunks of time identified with a name and justified as an effective point of entry into a segment of our past experience. Indeed, if we investigate even the most obvious structures of periodization, such as the twentieth century, we will find that historians argue as to when that century began and ended, because the 100 years between 1900 and 2000 are merely chronological markers: they do not constitute a unified period, cemented by shared institutions, events, or ideas. Most European historians will suggest that the century really began in 1914 with the outbreak of the First World War and ended in any one of a number of years, depending on what best explicates their analysis; so, questions need to be asked of such an organizing principle. It is necessary, then, to investigate some examples of periodization to assess how effective – or arbitrary – the definition of various of chunks of time can be.

The Example of the Middle Ages

Let's begin with the particularly vexing example of the European Middle Ages. When did they begin and when did they end? The Middle Ages, after all, hardly represent a clear set of temporal boundaries. And the answer to this kind of question will lead to important insights into the historian's assumptions and methods. If he or she decided to begin a general survey of the medieval world in 476 AD, we know that date recorded when the last 'Roman' Roman Emperor, Romulus Augustulus (*c.* 461–after 507 AD), ceased to reign. As a result, we as readers can assume that the historian accepted that there was a break in continuity between the Roman Empire and the establishment of 'barbarian' kingdoms in Italy and elsewhere in Europe. Although this is a widely accepted chronology, it is essentially based upon a narrow belief that political power should be privileged and ignores the reality that a great many of the defining institutions of the Roman world continued, such as the Christian religion and Church or the Latin language as the instrument of administration and even culture. Four hundred and seventy-six, then, provides a convenient but not necessarily useful beginning for the period known as the Middle Ages and the historian needs to explicate his or her reasoning for this decision, a discussion which usually results in the recognition that the date is a mere convention without much real insight into historical change.

Would it have been more useful to have chosen another moment to begin the Middle Ages: for example, 313 AD, the year of the Edict of Milan in which the emperor Constantine (*c.* 272–337 AD) recognized Christianity as an official religion of his empire? Medieval Europe was fundamentally characterized by Christianity and the Roman Church, so this could have worked. Or, what about 324 AD, the year that same Constantine founded Constantinople, his new capital in the east, beginning the Byzantine Empire, another prevailing structure that helped define medieval civilization? Could we argue for 800 AD when the Frankish king Charlemagne (*d.* 814) was crowned at Rome in the old basilica of St Peter as emperor, thereby creating a new imperial order in Europe? Of course any of these dates are possible; so the point I want to make is that any beginning date of any historical period will be to a degree arbitrary. However, that arbitrary choice can help the reader understand and appreciate the intention of the historian: what she or he finds significant, or what forces drive historical change, or how time can be coherently segmented, as long as the assumptions behind those divisions are clearly revealed.

So much for beginnings: what about endings? When did the Middle Ages really end? I have heard arguments for dates from the fourteenth century, based on the rise of towns and a money economy, to the seventeenth century and the beginning of the Scientific Revolution which provided a different means of assessing and acquiring knowledge. Many texts choose 1517, the year that saw Martin Luther's successful fragmentation of Christianity from a theoretically singular Roman confession into many mutually exclusive sects. Here, too, there is no right answer, as everything depends on those initial suppositions about what constitutes a historical period. If the Middle Ages are defined, as they often are, as the Age of Faith, then structural changes in the Church are of great significance, as are elaborations of theology; consequently, Luther's revolt is a reasonable choice. But, if you see the medieval world as a set of broader beliefs, methods, and structures, founded on an acceptance of divine involvement in human affairs, then the publication of René Descartes' (1596–1650) *Discourse on Method* of 1653 is a very plausible terminus because after the emergence of scientific method the ballast in the European mind shifted fundamentally, leading to a very different view of the universe and mankind's place in it.

Nevertheless, an Economic History of the Middle Ages might well begin with the establishment of landholding patterns that developed into feudalism. This would take the Middle Ages back into the final years of the late Roman Empire. Similarly, the choice of a terminal date could be any number of economic events or changes from the introduction of the gold florin by Florence in 1252 or the capture of Constantinople by the Turks in 1453, thereby complicating the European control of Mediterranean trade, or even Columbus's first voyage to the New World in 1492, an event that signalled the shift of the economic heart of Europe from the Mediterranean to the Atlantic seacoast. A professional historian can argue for any of these dates, and all of them would be useful, provided again that the author's intentions are made manifest in these choices.

Historical periodization is therefore only a set of convenient bookends for an analysis of events that can fit into a particular set of categories. It is incumbent upon the historian to make very clear what assumptions he or she is making about the time covered in his or her history and why those particular bookends were chosen. But, as in an any narrative or analysis, beginnings and endings matter, and a reader or student can learn a great deal about what the historian considers the most important factors driving historical change by how that historian identifies when a period in the past begins and ends and how it is defined.

Historical Periods Defined by Dynamic Ideas

How should we approach historical surveys that are not defined by traditional historical bookends often associated with important events but those which adhere to an organizing idea, process, or series of events? We have already seen an example of this in defining the Middle Ages as the Age of Faith. And there we saw that Christianity and the Roman Church operated as the glue that held that medieval chunk of time together for historians who use such a category. We can make similar observations about histories entitled Feudal Europe or any other number of ideas seen as the common elements linking events and evidence. But, what about categories of periodization which are more abstract, such as the Age of Exploration? When did this period begin and end – or has it ended at all?

Many historians have argued that the most significant event in early modern history is the expansion of Europe beyond its own continent, particularly the voyages that explored the newly discovered lands of the Americas and elsewhere. No doubt this is a compelling argument, but, again, when do these voyages begin and end? Do we include the Viking contacts with Canada's east coast half a millennium before Columbus? Do we include the explorations of the interior of Africa or the Arctic by Europeans in the nineteenth century? Should we include the exploration of space and the United States landing on the moon in recent times? All of these constitute exploration and many fall into similar patterns of human behaviour, but seldom do surveys of the Age Exploration contain them all. So, once again, any historian must establish why a particular period has been isolated and what principles were employed to define that chunk of time and why some events or evidence that appear to conform to those principles have been included and others not.

Again in European history, the seminal period defined as the Enlightenment has produced a huge number of studies. However, if you examine these texts you quickly note that some contain the Scientific Revolution of the seventeenth century, usually beginning with Galileo (Galileo Galilei, 1564–1642), while others do not. Some employ a broad lens which uses evidence from all across Europe, from the Russia of Catherine the Great (1729–1796) to Italian thinkers such as Beccaria (Cesare Beccaria, 1738–1794) and Vico (Giambattista Vico, 1668–1744); others limit their discussion to England and France, with some commentary on German Enlightenment thought, although often dependent on the core analysis of English and French material. In other words, the European Enlightenment is hardly a clearly focused historical period, even if almost any reader will have an idea what the book is about. This becomes an important consideration because it gives us a deeper understanding of a point we raised at the beginning of this book: historians disagree and they disagree on even the most fundamental elements of their craft, such as what constitutes a historical period and the chronological limits of each. At the same time, these differences and disagreements account for the profusion of books on what appears to be the same topic. Each one uses different evidence from different places and times to construct its analysis; and each offers another perspective on material that many think already heavily researched. A period as fundamental in the understanding of the history of Europe into modern times, such as the Enlightenment, can be therefore continually revisited and new implications and nuanced conclusions drawn. History is not a fixed enterprise but a changing kaleidoscope of scholarship, all of which share certain characteristics and elements, but each work of history is profoundly individualistic, with material unique to that study arranged according to principles equally unique to that historian.

Moreover, that same period has been called by other conventional names, such as the Age of Reason or Rationalism. The term Enlightenment is in fact an English translation of the French *éclaircissement*, which in itself implies recognition of the central role of the thinkers and writers of that nation in the formulation of rationalist thought. One might expect, then, that histories of the Enlightenment would privilege French texts from Descartes to Rousseau (Jean-Jacques Rousseau, 1712–1778), whereas the more broadly defined Age of Reason could equally accept British thinkers from Locke (John Locke, 1632–1704) to Adam Smith (1723–1790) or David Hume (1711–1776), as well as German and Italian writers. In short, in navigating the complexities of periodization, subtle differences in the titles of histories matter, as they can be clues to the author's choice of evidence and argument.

Therefore, in establishing periodization such as the Enlightenment or the Age of Reason, many historians use conventional temporal shorthand on the assumption that everyone will know what they mean. Another example would be a study entitled Revolutionary Europe or the Age of Revolution. Now, European history is full of revolutions; it would be hard to find a decade without one somewhere on the continent; so, why should there be an 'age' entitled 'revolutionary'; and why do we all understand that it refers to the years begun by the French Revolution of 1789 and largely concluded with the Congress of Vienna in 1814–1815? Academic convention and years of scholarship and school curricula have identified the French Revolution as

THE revolution. Indeed, when writing or speaking, most scholars and students simply refer to the French Revolution as the Revolution. Even the Russian Revolution of 1917 – which had a not dissimilar effect on the development of modern European history – is still given its geographical adjective, except in works that provide a context in which the event cannot be confused. Generalities are thus useful and conventions an effective shorthand. But, we must remember that these conventions merely lead us into the more detailed and deeper investigation of the period, at which point the unique perspective of the historian emerges.

Similarly, if we find a survey entitled the Age of Liberalism, what conclusions should we draw? Liberalism was a force that animated the entire European continent as well as the Americas and elsewhere in the nineteenth century; but the statesmen, political thinkers, and political platforms that identified themselves with Liberalism often meant quite different things. Certain principles were usually held in common, principles largely first described in England, from John Locke's *Second Treatise of Civil Government* in the late seventeenth century through Enlightenment thinkers to nineteenth-century writers such as Jeremy Bentham (1748–1832). Liberalism constituted the advocacy of a form of government based on the rule of law, individual rights, participatory democracy, freedom from arbitrary law or authority, and the primacy of private property and a free market economy. Whether in France, Germany, Russia, Italy or elsewhere in Europe, most of those who self-identified as liberals would agree with all of those statements. But, local contexts, traditions, institutions, and individual ambitions made a singular liberal confession that superseded national borders difficult. That meant that a liberal administration in Britain would see very different kinds of problems and solutions from one in France or Russia or even Spain. William Ewart Gladstone (1809–98), Benjamin Constant (1767–1830), or Wilhelm von Humboldt (1767–1835) would have a great deal to discuss had they found themselves together in a railway carriage, but the problems they saw in their own countries and the solutions they advocated would have still been very different.

Therefore, is it even useful to define a period like the Age of Liberalism? It is indeed because the basic principles of Liberalism in theory and in practice can be seen as a movement that spread across the continent and galvanized similar groups in society, especially the newly empowered and enriched urban middle classes, wherever they might be. Campaigns to extend the franchise, free trade, ensure equality under the law, social mobility, and the protection of individual property animated the political briefs of almost every liberal statesman, journalist, and engaged citizen. The differences in approach, emphasis, and means of effecting change might have been local but most of the ideas were universal, making the years between the 1840s and 1914 a period with some important shared coherent political and economic ambitions that merit being included in such a portmanteau period like the Age of Liberalism.

Much the same can be said about historical periods like the Age of Nationalism. The importance of nationalism in nineteenth- and twentieth-century Europe is profound. Any study of the nineteenth century will have to include lengthy sections on the unification of Italy and Germany, the growing nationalist sentiment in the Austrian (after 1867 Austro-Hungarian) Empire and the unfortunate development of unhealthy ideas of national or racial superiority in European thought. To understand Europe from the period of the French Revolutionary Wars to the present requires a clear appreciation of what has been called the most potent religion of the modern world.

From studies that identify a period like the Age of Nationalism, it naturally follows that the Age of Imperialism would represent its own historical moment. The forces that gave rise to nationalism, as well as the economic and industrial expansion of Europe, necessarily resulted in the vast expression of European power throughout the world, often with extremely unfortunate consequences. Although colonies had existed for centuries, the wholesale division of the world among a few great powers represented an entirely different level of oppression, particularly in Africa and Asia. Again, although ill-defined in time and place, any history of the Age of Imperialism would constitute a coherent and arresting study.

And, as I mentioned in an earlier chapter, the history of events depends very much on who is writing the history and his or her audience. A modern historian will deplore the imperial entitlement of Europeans towards the rest of the world, whereas a historian writing at the turn of the twentieth century would have a very different argument. The evidence employed would greatly separate such historians, and the conclusions drawn would be mutually exclusive. But, as I noted then, it is important that we have those old histories of the imperial period and that we read them in order to understand what Europeans were thinking and why they were behaving in what seems to us such a callous way.

Historical Periods Defined by Great Men or Women

How should we approach historical periods that are defined by an individual rather than a great event or series of linked events? Examples would be the Age of Napoleon (1769–1821), the Age of Elizabeth (1533–1603) or the Age of Louis XIV (1638–1715). It is obvious that periodization based upon the life of a single person would give some very clear indications of when that age began and ended. In the example of the Age of Elizabeth, we know that we are discussing England in the sixteenth century, as Elizabeth came to the throne in 1558 at the age of 25 and died in 1603. This is a considerable chunk of time and one with great implications for the history of not only England but all of Europe, as well as the Americas and beyond. But, what else might we discover from a period that historians characterize as dominated by an individual to the extent that she gave her name to a period of human history?

First, Elizabeth's life began not when she became queen but a quarter century earlier, and those 25 years were among the most tumultuous in her personal and her nation's history. She was the daughter of Anne Boleyn (1501–1536) and Henry VIII (1491–1547), in fact Anne's only living child; and Henry, because Anne did not provide a male heir, had her beheaded on trumped up charges of adultery (and hence treason), including incest with her brother. Henry VIII then did have a son with his next wife which removed Elizabeth and her half-sister Mary (1516–1558, Henry's daughter by his first wife, Catherine of Aragon) from the succession; but her half-brother's death in 1553 at 16 before he himself could secure a legitimate heir led to the accession of Mary, a devout Roman Catholic, who was pressured to execute Elizabeth as a threat to her throne, her religion, and her husband, Philip of Spain (1527–1598). It was only Mary's death in November of 1558 that ensured that Elizabeth would live and indeed become queen, and one of England's greatest rulers. Equally,

Elizabeth's decision not to marry and have an heir meant that the Tudor dynasty came to an end, leaving the throne to her cousin, James VI of Scotland, who became James I of England (1566–1625). Thus, the Age of Elizabeth requires a consideration of the Stuart dynasty as well, an analysis of the relationship between England and Scotland, and the execution of Mary, Queen of Scots (1587). People and families are complex.

This short potted history has a purpose. The Age of Elizabeth is more than that. It is not just the biography of a queen; and it includes necessarily the reigns of Henry VIII, Edward VI, and Mary I. The character, religion, politics, and allegiances of Elizabeth were forged largely by her experiences as a young woman during a very dangerous time. The life of an individual as an historical period is consequently a very important organizing category because important people like Elizabeth I encompass the life of her nation. From the moment of her birth, the Age of Elizabeth was being forged. Fortunately for her she lived and inherited the crown, allowing that remarkable woman to fulfil her destiny, or so the historian will claim.

A history of the Age of Elizabeth also obviously looks at events in those years from an English perspective. Thus, events on the continent will be shown to have been significant only when they affected the development of English policy and history; so, if you are interested in the Spanish Armada of 1588, the analysis will assume it as a great victory for English sea power. The Spanish – and indeed Catholic Europe – saw it quite differently. Even where the queen's few continental interventions had a positive impact on other states or peoples, it would be the English interpretation that would obtain. For example, England's entry into the revolt of the Netherlands against Spain was a major event for the Dutch; but the Age of Elizabeth would see it as an element of English policy and the consequences of that intervention assessed as such.

It is reasonable to ask whether a history built on the reign of a single queen – or any other individual – really still holds validity in modern historical research and writing. Certainly, the 'great man theory' has long been out of fashion and attributing events to the overarching personality of any one person – even a personality as powerful as Elizabeth, Napoleon, or Louis XIV – is reductive in a way that looks back to more traditional ways of analysing the past. Looking at England and the expressions of English political, economic, social, cultural, naval and military ambitions from the perspective of the Queen does provide a coherent structure and focus for very complicated events over a long period of time. The danger is, of course, to attribute too much influence to the crown, court, and centre and not enough to the margins, even if the model nevertheless has proved both popular and enduring.

The evidence that is assessed through the lens of a ruler will always privilege social, political and military elites, as they are the groups closest to the crown. To be sure, other classes or groups in society will appear but usually just as part of a broader picture driven by the policies of the court or the great man or woman. Consequently, the use of an individual personality to define a historical period is often useful and often engaging, as we all love interesting characters; but this kind of history has largely been superseded by other, more broadly based assessments of the past. Still, for the general reader or the fascinated student, personalities will always be a vehicle to attract them to an appreciation of the past and the world before our time.

On occasion, this model of periodization is extended to include an entire dynasty or two, especially in the writing of textbooks. Consequently, we find histories entitled Tudor England, specifically identifying the years between 1485 and 1603, the years the house of Tudor ruled England. If the title is Tudor Britain, it is understood that the other constituent parts of the Tudor crown, Wales and Ireland, will be included with England in some detail in the study of those years. Extending the title to Tudor and Stuart Britain indicates that England, Ireland, Wales, and Scotland will be studied between the years 1485 and 1714, that is, between the accessions of Henry VII and George I. Like the Age of Elizabeth, such extended studies still conform to the traditional analysis of history from the centre, dependent on the Crown and Parliament, and those groups and issues most important to these institutions. And, needless to say, such titles tend to define textbooks.

Historical Periods Defined by Specific Years or Centuries

The final chronological category of historical periodization that I will discuss is the obvious division of the past into years, decades, or centuries. This is the most visible of all the chunks of time through which historians can navigate their analysis of the past. A history entitled Europe in the nineteenth century is very clear: we know the area investigated and the years involved – or do we? Often there is a conventional shorthand at work here as well. Some histories begin with the Congress of Vienna (1814–1815) and continue until the outbreak of the First World War in 1914 on the assumption that this is a far more coherent and intelligent way of defining the century than simply using dates ending with zeros. And, there is much to be said for this position inasmuch as there are common elements that linked events in Europe between the defeat of Napoleon and the dissolution of the European state system as a result of the First World War (1914–1918). A parallel argument could be made, then, that the subsequent volume in such a history, the twentieth century, could begin in 1918; however, when it ended would be a cause of great debate, as we are still too close to events such as the fall of the Berlin Wall (9 November 1989), the collapse of the Soviet Union (1991), or the 9/11 terror attacks on New York City and Washington DC. Any of these terminal dates can be proposed for the end of the century, but we need a little more distance to decide which of these will prove the most transformative.

Some particular years have such an importance that they can constitute historical periods in themselves. This is true of 1848 which saw revolutions break out almost everywhere across Europe and led to eventual fundamental change in many of the major states of Europe. But, when looking at such a history what will be clear is that 1848 will be the hinge year of what must be a wider study. To understand why the events of 1848 happened, evidence from across the continent would have to be collected from the period of the Congress of Vienna to the aftermath of the 1848 revolts, an analysis that would vary from state to state. So, we know that the chronology will focus on the year of revolutions but we also know that what caused such widespread dissent and how the established authorities responded to it would equally need to be investigated and conclusions drawn.

Other momentous years have also spawned their own historical periods. 1914 is one example, 1789 another. When looking at single-year periodization with this degree of focus, it becomes clear that the year is a distillation of complex events which reached some degree of consummation in that year. The outbreak of the First World War began a cataclysm that changed not only Europe but the world and consequently this single year becomes a dramatic punctuation point and worthy of its own category. The coming of the French Revolution had the same effect, so the events that occasioned that explosion in 1789 merit such detailed discussion.

What all of this means is that a historian assessing events can divide the past into very large or very small chunks of time, depending on the subject and the method they choose to employ. Such variation is particularly useful to students and other scholars alike because these divergent methods of periodization permit readers to access evidence and analysis in different ways and at different depths. Focus is an element that all successful historians need to perfect and the fundamental decision about how to define the period under discussion, how that chunk of time is to be divided, investigated, and explicated, represents one of the first calls any author makes. Periodization in history is a necessary tool and one which reveals a great deal about the historian: his or her assumptions and methods and how the evidence will be used. Good students and researchers will vary their use of materials so that detailed, highly focused analysis can be viewed in a broader temporal or geographical context. And, this leads us to our next discussion of history categorized by geography.

The Study of History through Geographical Categories

Geographical categories can be identified in several ways. There are of course the political borders that define states. Consequently, historical libraries are full of histories of France, or Russia, or England. There are larger geographical regions with more than one political unit, such as histories of Italy in the Renaissance – that is, before unification – or a history of Eastern Europe. There are the histories of empires, such as Austria-Hungary, that constitute the amalgamation of many different nationalities and past or future independent kingdoms, such as Bohemia and Hungary. A history of Russia until very recent times would include now independent states, such as Ukraine, Estonia, and part of Poland, among a great many others that are now sovereign countries. And, Polish history must reflect the fact that the state itself did not exist from the end of the eighteenth century until 1918.

What all of this means is that the connection between Geographical History and sovereign political units is extremely complex, as borders change, composite states disintegrate, and national institutions vary according to the period under investigation. It is important, then, to realize that a nation, defined as a people with shared language, culture, and history, should not be equated with fixed political borders. Often this will require some preliminary knowledge to sort out the composite nature of the many countries which are the product of long histories of conquest, dynastic inheritance, or assimilation.

Even so, it is extremely important to study states in the past as political units, because decisions taken in the capitals and courts of these composite states had important implications for all those living under their jurisdiction. Consequently, it might be more useful to discuss, for example, a history of the Polish people, rather than a history of Poland, to reflect the partition of the old Polish kingdom among Russia, Prussia, and Austria; but the identification of territory with nation is old and deeply ingrained. For the clearest examination of the history of a particular geographical area, then, it is important to connect to a specific historical period. Should we talk about the history of Spain before the military and dynastic unification of the Iberian Peninsula late in the fifteenth century? Should we see Italy, as Metternich did, as only a geographical expression before unification in 1861? And, in this example, even that date is unsatisfactory because Venice and its territories were not acquired until 1866 and Rome and the remainder of the papal states not until 1870 and Trentino-Alto Adige, Gorizia, and Trieste only in 1918.

Geography, then, is complex and confusing in Europe. And, should we generalize by associating many countries into traditional geographical areas? What are the Balkans, for example? We can identify the several states that occupy that geographical space, but what is the real advantage of associating them into a larger territory? Some of these nations follow Orthodox Christianity, like Serbia and Greece; some are Catholic, like Croatia; and one, Bosnia, is largely Muslim, and another, Albania, heavily Muslim. Some were part of the Ottoman Empire until late in the nineteenth or even early twentieth centuries and some were part of the Austro-Hungarian Empire or old kingdom of Hungary. Today, most of the Balkan states are part of the European Union, but not all; and some still bear the trauma of the terrible wars and ethnic cleansing that resulted from the disintegration of the former state of Yugoslavia in the 1990s. Some refuse to recognize the borders of others and some maintain a heightened tension as a consequence of historical burdens and perceived wrongs. So, should there be a history of the Balkans? Indeed there should because of all of these factors. The complex and bloody history of the geographical area can only be clarified by investigating the past in terms of a shared, even if hostile, experience. Understanding will come from studying that experience and the past and present interaction among those small nations that find themselves living in such close proximity. History is often messy and its writing is never a simple linear record. If we strive to understand the past and present and acquire some insight into what the future might hold, then political or national isolation and particularistic studies are not the answers. Geography is more than a congregation of territory: it is history and memory and hence needs a broad focus and a wide perspective.

History as Chunks of Space

The connection with the writing of history and a defined territory is almost anthropological. There has ever been a powerful connection between a people and the land they inhabit, even to the point of perverting the nature of community and identity itself, as represented by the Nazi cult of blood and soil. History has often claimed mythical spaces, spaces that cannot be compromised, regardless how much time has altered that original belief. Think, for example, of the Serbian obsession with Kosovo, where they lost a battle against the Turks in the fourteenth century (1389) and where the majority of the population is now Albanian. This territory became so infused with historical myth, nationalist fervour, and uncompromising diplomacy that an unnecessary and debilitating war resulted. History, then, can sanctify geography.

Much the same can be said about the Italian irredentist movement of the nineteenth and early twentieth centuries. The idea of an 'unredeemed' part of the national homeland drove many statesmen into bellicose postures, with little reasonable consideration of the implications at the time. I could go on; but the principle should now be clear that 'national' or nationalist histories are often tainted with an assumption that there is chunk of territory that is the natural, historic, and consequently non-negotiable part of the very identity of a people. Historians too often in the past have fallen into this unhappy company and perpetuated a sense of historic wrongs inflicted upon a people by others. In the nineteenth century, nationalist movements could therefore use history to identify enemies, defined by their holding of traditional territory or ethnic groups in subjection; and such work had a powerful effect on the decisions of statesmen who vowed to correct that injustice. Wars were fought and populations uprooted or 'cleansed', usually with devastating results for all concerned.

Consequently, it is important for the historian to know these elements of history, defined by myth and geography, a history usually characterized as historic injustice to be avenged or redressed. Only then can we really understand the forces at work that drove historical judgment, military campaigns, and political platforms. Students and scholars need to know exactly what territory the history is describing and when, as well as assess whether the historian has adopted national – or nationalist – positions. Myth and fervent nationalism have a way of deforming evidence, creating an historical vision that is more often polemic than balanced analysis.

There are, however, certain chunks of space that lend themselves extremely well to detailed and exceptionally valuable historical study. Consider, for example, the Victoria County Histories, begun in the nineteenth century (1899), in which every county in England is studied. This degree of focus is an excellent way to acquire deep insight into a relatively small area and to see its history in terms of the broader perspectives of culture. Similarly, Urban History can delve deeply into the development of the urban spaces of cities and towns. Urban History constitutes one of the genres of history which we will investigate in more detail in the next chapter; but cities constitute a chunk of space and one that benefits from such an analysis.

A term students and scholars occasionally encounter, especially when looking at ancient, Renaissance or even nineteenth-century local histories, is *chorography*; and, indeed, the term is enjoying in some small ways something of a rehabilitation. Simply put, chorography is a kind of regional historical study based on detailed maps and surveys that offer deep insight into every aspect of a small part of the world. Besides maps, charts, and surveys, chorography often includes images – or photographs – of landscape, topography, and urban settlement. Roads, waterways, bridges, fords, and other elements are noted to explain the development of that very circumscribed chunk of space over time. The tradition began with the ancient geographers, such as Ptolemy (Claudius Ptolemaeus; *c.* 90–*c.* 168 AD), and was revived in the Renaissance enthusiasm for ancient models. Of these, the most famous practitioners were William Camden (1551–1623) in England (see his *Britannia* of 1580) and Leandro Alberti (1479–1552), in his *Discrittione di Tutta Italia* (1550), in Italy. In the nineteenth century, German historiography found chorography a useful tool in local studies following unification.

Similarly, micro histories often investigate very small territories, such as a town or village and its environs, a particular feudal manor, the property of a single family, or even part of a larger city or county. These kinds of local history often offer great depth and insight into a particular place, especially if the surviving evidence is rich and continuous. Tracing landholding patterns in a village or manor, following the vagaries of a family's property or assessing how a borough reflected changing social, economic, and political circumstances can yield very satisfying results. Here, the small piece of a larger unit can afford an insight into how communities change over time and can offer either support or a corrective to broader generalities. Micro histories are becoming increasingly popular, as the limitation in space permits a much greater scope of extremely detailed study over time and through many lenses.

Thus, what we have discussed in this chapter is how the study of history requires divisions, either in time (periodization) or space; and any kind of generalization about any aspect of the past necessitates an analysis of how and why change occurred. Consequently, the division of the past requires certain decisions concerning the principles which were used to explicate those divisions. And, as I hope this chapter indicated, many of these principles will be to some degree arbitrary and therefore they need clear explication because the assumptions, methodology, and choice of evidence will have a defining effect on the conclusions. Geographical or temporal categories can be misleading and consequently need clarification to guide the reader into the nature of the research. A history of Poland is not the same as a history of the

Polish People; and a history of Renaissance Italy will investigate very different years from a history of Renaissance England.

It is the historian's responsibility to justify what categories he or she used in writing that work, and what exactly his or her book is really about. The resulting variety in material, methodology, and analysis, however, adds to our understanding of the past and provides a richer mine of evidence to discover how change operated over time and across space. No two history books are ever the same because every historian interprets these fundamental divisions of time and space in different ways, and we are much the wiser for this diversity in perspective.

5

The Many and Various Forms of Historical Writing

The More Traditional Structures

I have suggested that there are a great many ways in which history can be divided. The previous chapter suggested that the two most basic categories of temporal and geographical history have been central to the historian's craft since history was first written. As the discipline matured, however, new ways of interpreting the past developed. Often these were responses to changes in how society itself was analysed, reflecting contemporary values and perspectives on politics, economics, race, gender, and culture, just to note the most obvious. What I am suggesting, then, is that history is a glass through which the historian's world sees itself. This, naturally, can lead to distortions of the past, as it is now too often viewed not according to its own principles and experiences but only through the eyes of the society in which the historian works and lives. This, nevertheless, has useful and positive consequences: it means that history remains a vibrant and engaged discipline; and that change over time is recorded both in the work and through the work. It also helps explain why historians so often fail to agree: they are writing with competing or even mutually exclusive perspectives. As I noted in the first chapter, the study of history is really the study of historians.

Consequently, when we think of the many sub-disciplines and ideological and methodological varieties of historical writing today we must remember that each is addressing a particular audience with its own methods, expectations, and vocabulary. These highly focused

The Experience of History, First Edition. Kenneth Bartlett.

discussions permit us to investigate elements of the past that have been ignored or even vilified. They allow different methodologies to discuss heterodox ideas or practices on their own terms, rather than as a part of a larger, often more traditional, narrative. And, the very recognition of these newer categories of history validates their subjects and the material used in their explication.

Thus, the proliferation of new genres of history does not represent a fragmentation of the discipline but rather a more nuanced and focused way to approach the study of the past. The various perspectives that have developed over the last decades have greatly enriched the study of history; and all of us, both student and scholar, are the better for it. Our appreciation of the past has grown with detailed studies that investigate aspects of human experience previously ignored or even considered taboo; and for this we should be grateful. The development of civilization is not a linear or a singular process: it is diverse in its material and broad in its reach. So, let's celebrate some of these genres of history by discussing them severally. It would be a book in itself to define in detail all of these methodologies, so what follows is a commentary on both the traditional and the more recent – even transgressive – approaches to our shared past.

The Chronicle

We have already looked at the most traditional means of discussing the past when we looked at histories structured chronologically and geographically. But, there are other, even older ways, of recording the past. The chronicle, for example, has been a way of listing events which an individual or institution believes worth preserving. A common historical genre in the Middle Ages, this means of recording history reflects a desire to preserve some knowledge of the past, often for practical purposes. It was important to know when certain events occurred, events such as the dates of kings, bishops, abbots, or saints. Moments of danger or salvation, like invasions, battles won or lost, freedom from threats like famine, plague, or flood all provided shared past experience for a community and one which linked it with those who had gone before.

Usually, the chronicle is a simple list, chronologically structured, that has very little by way of analysis or commentary. Also, chronicles are seldom the result of deep research, more often dependent on oral history, earlier chronicles, and legends. Sometimes, there is an element of research, particularly in monastic or town chronicles, where some evidence might be conserved. In these instances, the chronicler, whether an amateur or an official tasked with the compilation of the material, would have access to documents and other sources of information. In general, however, even here there is little interpretation or judgment: events are merely recorded.

Chronicles that are local in nature will almost always intersperse entries of wide significance with those that are largely of interest only to the immediate community. For example, a medieval chronicle might record the death of a king and the succession of his heir immediately after an entry naming a new novice inducted into the monastery. A fire that destroyed the monastic kitchen could share an entry with the news of the death of a pope or the arrival of visitors from the bishop. In an urban chronicle, major events such as the lifting of a siege or plague will alternate with notices of the deaths of individual citizens or occasionally even members of the chronicler's own family. Here, too, hearsay, legend and imperfect information will be fused with some documentary material, perhaps laws promulgated or a charter granted for the city or the cost of bread.

This is in no way to imply that chronicles are not extremely useful instruments for modern students and scholars: they again provide insight into what a particular community or individual thought was important and worth recording. Sometimes, the only clear date we have for an event is found in a chronicle; and the chronicler's descriptions of attacks, floods, or famines all provide necessary information for our piecing together knowledge of the past.

More than with other historical records, chronicles must be used carefully. The intention of the chronicler was not to provide objectively correct information to be used as evidence by future historians. The purpose is very different indeed: to increase the fame of the religious order or monastery, to praise and claim authority for a particular town or even ruling family, or to identify the working of divine providence. What it was not designed to achieve was an accurate, balanced historical record of events based on the rigorous use of evidence. Still, without chronicles our understanding of large parts of the past would be poorer.

Political History

The ancients believed that history was a record of the political and military deeds of great men, an idea that was revived in the Renaissance. Consequently, Political History constitutes a venerable and large category of traditional histories. These vary, obviously, in detail and subject matter but most record the work of kings and queens, princes, parliaments, governments, and other political institutions. The premise is that whoever made the law shaped society and enjoyed a privileged position in that society. To know, therefore, the deeds and intentions of the powerful was to understand the nations and societies they ruled.

Modern historians hardly accept this perspective today; nevertheless, there is an important need to follow the definition of power and to access the operations and principles of governing individuals and institutions. We today must know how a state functioned to make judgments about how it changed over time and why. Powerful men – as they were usually men – exercised authority according to certain principles and structures that can be effectively elucidated by studying the documents of Political History and investigating the relationships among men, ideas and government. Thus, traditional as it is, Political History is still written and continues in many forms. It can take the form of political biography, such as the life of a king, president, or prime minister, told through the political legacy of power. It can be an Institutional History: for example, a history of the British House of Commons, a royal council, or the Democratic Party. This is the history of power in its traditional form, exercised by traditional elites. To perform in the political arena is to automatically admit men or women into privileged company, whether they want it or not. It can be highly focused on short periods of time and specific places, such as the four-year term of an American President or the brief tenure of power of a prime minister, or it can discuss political or institutional life over vast distances of time.

To a great degree, Political History is a point of view, inasmuch as it directs the student or scholar to the operation and results of government. The lens is the lens of politics and legal authority, of powerful personalities and control of the agenda of legislation. So, although most modern Political Histories will include elements of Economic, Social, Intellectual, and Military History in their narratives, the primary perspective will always be the political.

Diplomatic History

For this reason I will include other subgenres of history within Political History, but with reservations. For example, Diplomatic History is the exercise of political agendas outside as well as within the nation under study; but these are usually driven by national political considerations. The kinds of evidence and documents used in Diplomatic History – often from more than one nation – can vary from standard Political History but diplomacy and politics are invariably impossible to separate. Still, there are specific practices and methods associated with diplomacy that justify its own category of historical research and analysis; consequently, let's recognize it as its own field, closely associated with politics.

Moreover, there are certain elements of Institutional History which derive from specific interests in many kinds of historical writing, and Diplomatic History is a good example. When, for example, a historian is investigating the negotiations of the Treaty of Westphalia (1648), the Congress of Vienna (1814–1815), the Paris 1919 Treaties (the Treaty of Versailles and the other instruments negotiated at the end of the First World War), the League of Nations, or the United Nations, a method of analysis to broaden his or her historical perspective and employ evidence from many participants is required. Thus, it is not enough to deal with the great personalities informing these events, men such as Cardinal Richelieu (Armand du Plessis de Richelieu, 1585–1642), Prince Metternich (Klemens Wenzel Nepomuk Lothar, Prince von Metternich-Winneburg-Beilstein, 1773–1859) or President Woodrow Wilson (1856–1924): a historian must look beyond individuals and into the structures that allowed such complex diplomacy to operate and the factors that drove the various agendas of the many participants.

Consequently, the institutional structures – and documentary evidence they preserve – of many states must be fully understood. For example, the functioning of the British Foreign Office, the Quai d'Orsay (the French Foreign Office), the US State Department, and the various branches of the League of Nations and the UN all contribute to the complex interaction among nations, individuals, and supranational organizations to define how diplomacy worked in the past and how it functions in the present. A great many skills are needed, especially a good command of foreign languages, to ensure that the many competing policies and ambitions of a great many states are effectively investigated and valid conclusions drawn. Diplomatic History, then, does constitute an extension of Political History but not just of one nation, and it is this multifaceted international research that delivers its greatest challenge.

Legal History

Much the same can be argued for Legal History, that is, the analysis of how the law was defined, legislated, enforced, and practised. Legal History is also often the story of institutions, such as courts, the bar, and policing; but it is also equally an investigation of government or monarchy: the elected representatives or royal authorities who determined what defined the law. Indeed, the investigation of how the law and legal theory changed over time is often an excellent barometer of how that society operated and identified and structured its basic principles. Whether the law operated as an independent jurisdiction, free from powerful interference and predicated on the principles of fairness and equal treatment, can usually be seen as an indication of how free that society was and how able its citizens were to criticize or oppose the established order. Legal History is thus to a degree Constitutional History because in those states that enjoyed a written or unwritten constitution or basic law such rights are enshrined. The degree to which the constitution is breached in practice or upheld tells us much about the political, intellectual, and economic reality in any country at any time. Add to this the study of punishment – from arrest to torture to prisons to the existence of capital punishment – and the character of a state can emerge. It has often been observed that the true soul of a nation is reflected in how its treats its prisoners; hence such knowledge is essential.

Military History

A not dissimilar case can be made for Military History. The celebrated nineteenth-century Prussian theorist of war, Carl von Clausewitz (1780–1831), remarked that war is the continuation of politics (or diplomacy) by other means. And, as we have noted, ancient historians linked political and military events, accomplished by great men, as the appropriate areas of interest for those concerned with the past. However, Military History has established its own category of research and analysis. To be sure there are often references to diplomacy or politics – and to diplomats and politicians – as well as monarchs and governments; but the analysis of tactics, strategy, logistics, command, and equipment has required a much more focused line of enquiry. Indeed, Military History is sufficiently complex that it has fragmented into subgenres of its own. Especially in modern times, the need to understand the complex technologies of warfare on land, sea, and air, the central role of financing what has become an extremely expensive operation, and the fundamental principles of organizational behaviour have all contributed to the challenging nature of Military History. What had been to the ancients the study of great men engaged in great deeds of daring, heroism, and patriotism has now been developed into an interrelated web of factors which all need explication. The kinds of evidence are varied and complex and the arguments subtle and demanding. In many ways, Military History has developed in parallel to the now enormous complexity of the state itself, something that von Clausewitz would have grasped at least in principle.

Economic History

Like Political History, Economic History is a complex field that is composed of many elements, all of which are important in the understanding of how economic forces drove change in the past. Although identified as significant with the rise of economic theory in the Enlightenment, Economic History has much deeper roots. Even the ancients recognized the indissoluble connection between money and power, whether political or military. Cicero (Marcus Tullius Cicero, 106–43 BC) stated in his orations (*The Philippics*) against Mark Antony (83 BC–30 AD) that the sinews of war were infinite money. The economic policies of Roman emperors were discussed by classical historians; and these concerns were rehearsed later in the Renaissance, especially in cities like fifteenth-century Florence, where mercantile policy and wealth defined the nature of the republic. Consequently, when reviewing history at any period and in almost every genre, there will always be an element of Economic History. When Mr Jorkin in the 1951 film based on Charles Dickens's *A Christmas Carol* stated, 'Control the cashbox and you control the world', he was reflecting a belief that forms a primary part of the western tradition.

Economic History is in part the history of money: its value, manipulation, accumulation, and expenditure. The narratives of history, then, take on a very different character when investigated through such a lens. For example, major moments in medieval European history can be seen to have been the introduction of the Florentine florin in 1252 or the Venetian ducat in 1284; and significant events, such as the crusades, can be interpreted not in terms of religious conflict but through the desire to control the long-distance luxury trade with the east, the growing population of the European knightly class, and the expansion of shipping among the Italian mercantile republics. Indeed, such examples can be used to explain the remarkable expansion of wealth and power of the Italian cities in the Middle Ages and Renaissance, acknowledging the role that economic policy played in their development, and to account for the vigorous experiments in centralized state building by monarchs in northern Europe.

The kinds of evidence for Economic History are often very rich, at least from the Middle Ages onwards. Money must be accounted for; trade leaves detailed records; taxation reflects official policy, as does the value of currency; expenditures are noted; customs and excise taxes are levied; and banks lend and accumulate capital. The documentation in fact can often be overwhelming and requires a very sophisticated eye to use properly. Moreover, economic documents are, as I suggested in my discussion of evidence, sometimes misleading, as recording the truth is not always in everyone's financial interest. Furthermore, currencies often fluctuated wildly in value, so how much money are we really talking about? Fictions, such as hidden fees or interest, are occasionally built into accounts to circumvent the religious injunction against lending money at interest (usury). Profit might be hidden behind the granting of land, or monopolies or special privileges. Records might not be continuous, so speculation is sometimes needed to ensure a coherent argument; or one part of a ledger survives and the others do not, making it difficult for the modern historian to balance old accounts. The value of merchandise fluctuated, as did the costs of transportation and production as a result of tangential events such as war, piracy, plague, company failure, or even market manipulation. The economic historian must correct for all of these and more, once the variables become clear.

But, a particular challenge is to relate the economic analysis of times past to the other elements of historical research. Currency valuation, the levels of taxation and their yields, state expenditure, company or personal wealth, and economic influence, as well as trade, manufacturing, and banking – whether under the control of individuals, families, companies or the state – all play roles in the study of change over time. These elements often reflected other factors dependent on the analysis of money and wealth, factors which link Economic with Social and Political History. As money has the ability to seep into every crevice of any society and become one of the most powerful engines of change, it is difficult, if not impossible, to fully isolate Economic History from other elements in research. It cannot really stand alone, although again the economic historical perspective needs the unity and coherence of adhering to an economic perspective, allowing those other factors to reveal themselves as products of the primary means of analysis.

Political, Military, and, as we will see, Social and Cultural History all are part of the analysis. Money, currency, and trade require policies in place to regulate and even drive the economy; wars make huge demands on the economy of any state and its citizens; money is also the lubricant for social mobility, permitting individuals and families to rise, often to great heights. The Medici began as bankers but by the sixteenth century were Grand Dukes of Tuscany and produced two queens of France (Catherine de'Medici, wife of Henry II, and Marie de'Medici, wife of Henry IV). Important offices in the church and state were very often sold, allowing wealthy families to buy their ways into the nobility or the hierarchy of the church. And, money is an absolute requisite for the patronage of culture. The creation of art presupposes surplus capital; without a positive economic environment, the efflorescence of culture is limited and more difficult.

Money, therefore, with fiscal policy and economic practice, forms one of the platforms on which society is built, No history can altogether ignore economic issues, as money is the primary lubricant of any complex society. Consequently, Economic History forms an essential element of the historian's brief.

Subgenres of Economic History

More recently, specific subgenres of Economic History have developed, reflecting both the importance of the enterprise and the popular interest in such subjects. Company histories, for example, have proliferated, together with the stories of families who acquired great wealth through business and finance. Investment histories look at the means of accumulating capital, especially after the introduction of stock exchanges in the Low Countries in the sixteenth century. The history of money itself and even the history of value (what is something worth and to whom and when) have added insights into how we view the past. And, as a natural projection of these subjects, recently there have emerged excellent studies on the history of shopping, making the retail consumer part of the great economic transformation.

Closely associated with Economic History are works on large subjects that contain a huge amount of economic analysis because of the role that capital played in that area. For example, any history of the industrial revolution must have a great deal of analysis on the accumulation of capital. This is an excellent example of how Technological, Economic, Social, and Political History merge into a multifaceted study of a historical phenomenon: industrialization. It is hardly accidental, then, that Karl Marx's (1818–1883) theory of historical change, dominated as it is by the rise of capitalism and its antithesis, the industrial working class (proletariat), is in essence a study of Economic History. Marxist historiography, therefore, will always be fundamentally infused with an analysis of economic factors; this is inescapable in the Marxist methodology, and it indicates how from the nineteenth century Economic History has become a powerful instrument in elucidating the past. A historian certainly does not need to be a Marxist to recognize this; but in the Marxist analysis it is essential.

Cultural and Intellectual History

Cultural and Intellectual History are by their very nature interdisciplinary, and make considerable demands on the interpretative skills of the historian; but these genres of research provide critical insights by revealing necessary information about a historical period by assessing what ideas were current and driving change in every facet of life, and how a great many of these ideas did not originate in works of political, social, or economic theory but in literature, or even music and art. Although many scholars separate Cultural and Intellectual History into two distinct categories, my own belief is that they are indissoluble. The History of Ideas presupposes instruments to develop, spread, discuss, and teach those ideas, which is very often the role of culture, both through institutional culture and through more popular cultural media, like novels, plays, and even music. So, I will discuss culture and ideas together.

The role of ideas as the engines of change over time has been recognized from the time of the ancients. In discussions of the Peloponnesian War (431–404 BC), for example, the sharp differences between the intellectual and cultural models of the Athenians and Spartans were correctly recognized. Kings, statesmen, and orators throughout recorded history are identified as the creators or creatures of prevailing or revolutionary ideas; and policy itself is impossible to define without understanding the intellectual assumptions that lie behind them.

European history is full of examples of the power of ideas. Think of the Scientific Revolution and Enlightenment and the role played by men who had little or no interest in changing the political, social, religious, or economic structures of their worlds but nevertheless forged the platform for the most fundamental change in all of these things: René Descartes, Isaac Newton (*d.* 1727), Galileo Galilei, just to note the most obvious. There were others whose books were directed towards changing the fundamental principles of their societies but through the application of reason and logic, men such as John Locke (*d.* 1704), Voltaire (François-Marie Arouet de Voltaire, *d.* 1778), the Baron de Montesquieu (Charles-Louis de Secondat, Baron de La Brède et de Montesquieu, *d.* 1755), Adam Smith (*d.* 1790), and Jean-Jacques Rousseau (*d.* 1778). And often these kinds of intellectual catalysts for historical change were fully open about their intentions. After all, Denis Diderot (*d.* 1784) and Jean'd'Alembert (Jean-Baptiste le Rond d'Alembert, *d.* 1783), the editors of the massive French encyclopaedia, printed on the title page that the purpose was to change the general mode of thought; and that led to changing principles which animate political, economic, and social change, manifested in the French Revolution. Ideas matter and only the most foolish historian would not admit to their role in effecting dramatic change.

What many of those historians who feel uncomfortable with Intellectual History argue is that the connections between current ideas and political, social, religious, or economic change are hard to evidence. Was there a particular idea, or book or individual which convinced the leaders of their communities to act? Were these ideas perhaps not just 'in the air' and were not the solutions and the problems evident to everyone? Voltaire, for example, wrote little by way of real political theory: he was a satirist and a polemicist, so what role did he really play in the coming of the French Revolution? Such arguments are hardly convincing. For real change to occur, men and women need to be able to imagine an alternative to the world as they knew it. That was the contribution of writers like Locke, Montesquieu, and Rousseau. And, they needed to accept that even those institutions that were most deeply imbedded into the collective consciousness of a people and the traditions of the community were seriously, even fatally, flawed and hence needed fundamental change, institutions like the Catholic Church in *ancien régime* France and the Bourbon monarchy itself.

Those who neglect Intellectual and Cultural History often do so because some historians feel inadequate in using literary or philosophical texts as historical evidence and even more inadequate in assessing cultural productions – painting and music, for example – as instruments for change. But, historians must do this, because by reading what those influential citizens of another time were reading, or listening to, or watching is a powerful way to access their experience of the world, the ideas animating it, and the problems or solutions identified. It was not an accident, then, that the royal censorship in *ancien régime* France, or the Index of Forbidden Books in the Roman Church, or the thought control of every totalitarian dictatorship anywhere in the world existed. They knew the power of ideas and culture, so there was the recognition that they must be completely controlled or silenced.

Students and scholars, then, must learn how to use literature in particular but also music and art, to enter the mind of the past. These are not easy documents to decode, because the very existence of censorship in the state and church requires the use of oblique or hidden messages, complex fictions, or metaphorical constructions. These things are not as immediate to us as they were to those living when the text was written; and allusions or references can be lost in the fog of time. But, these kinds of records provide extremely important – indeed necessary – insights into the minds of men and women long gone but who accomplished great things. The confidence that great changes and a better vision of the world were possible often resulted from the lessons of literature and art, so we must learn to use this evidence as well.

Many readers will wonder why this discussion does not contain sections on the History of Science and the History of Medicine. These are legitimate, well developed, and sophisticated studies of the intellectual contours of the past as seen through past scientific and medical knowledge and practice; and indeed historians of science and medicine often inhabit history departments in western universities. Nevertheless, I am not making separate distinctions for these sub-disciplines because in some ways they represent the prefaces to the modern study of medicine and science and in others they constitute chapters in any Intellectual History of Europe. This is not to disparage these significant areas of research but to note that Intellectual History includes all aspects of the mind of the past. Moreover, until quite recently, science was defined as Natural Philosophy and was infused with the principles of Aristotle and the philosophers of the ancient and early modern world. Medicine was very often associated with the Arts faculty in medieval and Renaissance universities because the texts were Galen (Aelius Galenus or Claudius Galenus, 130–200 AD) and other early physicians who wrote in Greek and Latin. So, the History of Science and Medicine are very much described here but in the general interdisciplinary category of Intellectual History, where they really belong.

Church or Confessional History

In many ways the Institutional History of churches is quite different from confessional histories. A scholarly study of the Roman Church in the Middle Ages, for example, presupposes some knowledge of Catholic theology; otherwise, such a history would be difficult if not impossible to write, given the obvious need to investigate how elements of faith informed church office and determined ecclesiastical organization. However, a history of the Catholic Faith would be something different again, as doctrinal knowledge would be central to any such study; and, it could be argued, that confessional allegiance would make such a task easier, if only because of the subtle details of belief and practice that such a history would require.

Institutional Church History can really be written by anyone of any faith or none, as it requires a balanced and often critical assessment of elements of that story that might not come easily to those committed to a particular confession. In many ways the history of a church or part of a church, such as a specific episcopal see or monastery, or a church in national context, such as a study of the church in France under the *ancien régime*, is a history like any other and demands the same level of rigorous scholarship and assessment of evidence. Often this evidence is extremely rich because of the church's need for records, the often highly literate and trained personnel, and the local traditions or privileges attached to specific parts of the church. What often emerges is an Institutional History that almost parallels that of the secular state in which the church is located. Each had its own, separate legal system and courts, means of taxation, ownership of property, a hierarchy of officers with defined tasks, and complex, subtle policies that usually went beyond matters of faith. In the case of the Roman Church the history is further complicated by the relationship between the various 'national' churches and the papal centre of the church in Rome. Similar complexities can be found in reformed Christian churches as well but concentrated mostly on relations with the local secular powers.

A problem exists in older church histories, inasmuch as a strong confessional allegiance often informs the scholarship. In some instances this is vituperative, attacking the structure and practices of one church from the committed perspective of another. Like older works on imperialism or slavery, these old church histories have little scholarly value, except as insights into the minds of the historians who wrote them and the uncompromising, indeed bigoted, ideas they shared with many of their contemporaries. Because the research is designed to impugn rather than enlighten, such old histories must be used with great care; however, as with other texts with unpleasant messages, these are extremely useful for modern students and scholars to enter into the minds of historians who surrendered their objectivity and academic integrity to prejudice.

Confessional histories are almost always written by believers or, occasionally, by those who have fallen away from a faith. These kinds of histories are again useful from a cultural or intellectual perspective, providing a means of access to deeply held convictions or into the functions of institutions that operate according to different principles. The role of divine providence, revelation, and inspired leadership tend to be the dominant characteristics of confessional histories and there is a kind of spiritual tautology at work in them: things are the way they are because that is how they are meant to be. Here, too, students and scholars must be wary, as the selective use of evidence and the operation of forces outside human causality can result in questionable conclusions that cannot be trusted.

Jewish History

Jewish History presents a unique and more complex problem in European history, as the Jews were not confined any one place but are found everywhere on the continent at some time. They were in the community often but not of it; they were by law and custom outsiders, driven inward, and only in the most unusual of circumstances permitted to fully participate in the life of their host village, city or nation. Moreover, Jews were not just defined by a set of religious beliefs: they had a culture of their own, their own communities and customs that make them in many ways a nation in themselves. This idea of a nation in diaspora will be something I will return to, as diaspora studies have become a genre of history in itself; but, after the campaigns of the Roman Emperor Titus in 70 AD and the expulsion of the Jews from Palestine, the Jews represent the defining model of a diaspora, events described in ancient times by the Romanized Jewish historian Flavius Josephus (37–*c.* 100 AD). What is remarkable is how Jewish belief was sustained in a relatively coherent fashion, despite not having any central structure to maintain uniformity. Certainly there were local differences in practice, dress, some customs, and even language; but the essential elements of Judaism remain fixed. This was because it was a religion of the book and that book was the determining instrument for the Jewish community's cultural and social as well as religious identification.

That said, it is usual to study the history of the Jews in the context of the nations they inhabited and the peoples among whom they lived. There are, of course, some very good and important histories of the Jews or the Jewish people; but more often their history appears through local evidence: the Jews in Venice, France or Hungary, for example. Occasionally this history can be terrible, reflecting badly on our judgments on the Christians around them, exemplified by the expulsion of the Jews from Spain in 1492, or the pogroms in Russia, or in its most chilling aspect of the Holocaust perpetrated by the Nazis. Besides these tragic events, there were other, if less lethal, humiliations: Jews often had to live in designated areas, wear distinctive dress, were restricted in what professions they could practise, and the degree to which they could interact with the Christian community around them. Often, then, the story of the Jews in Europe is a narrative of persecution and injustice. Nevertheless, this history forms part of the development of Europe and must be confronted, regardless of how unpleasant it might be. Furthermore, like Church or Religious History, Jewish History need not be written only by Jews, provided that a gentile historian understands enough of Jewish practice, language, and culture to appreciate the subtleties. As with all such history, objectivity can be a useful tool.

Histories of other Heterodox Religious Communities

Jews were not the only persecuted or marginalized communities within the history of Europe. Any list would be long and many of these suffered an equally cruel fate, at least until the Holocaust. For example, Christian heretics, those who set their own beliefs in opposition to the orthodox teachings of Catholicism or the Protestant confessions, represent communities at odds with the world around them and suffered accordingly. The medieval crusades against the Cathars or Albigensians of Southern France in the thirteenth century resulted in terrible slaughter and torture; the religious wars between Calvinists and Catholics in France in the second half of the sixteenth century were among the most savage on the continent; Protestant persecutions of Anabaptists were exemplary in their viciousness; and all confessions preached hatred and destruction against Muslims. What I am saying is that writing the histories of the persecuted and marginalized requires looking both into the group persecuted and the motives and practices of the persecutors. Much of it was born of ignorance and fear; but much was inspired by those who believed that only one religion – their religion – could operate in any place. Expulsions, slaughters, forced conversions, or daily humiliations often characterized the stories of these marginalized communities, even in places, like Venice, where they enjoyed somewhat more freedom than elsewhere. Europeans have never been very open until very recently to confessions other than their own; so the stories of minorities are usually the history of violence against them.

Here we must be careful of the evidence. Much of the documentation that survives comes from the persecutors: trials, arrests, expropriation of property, and expulsions. Not enough remains of the voices of the persecuted to form a complete picture of their lives. It is not that history is told by the victors; rather, it is that those persecuting others had access to the offices of the state, including the military and the law; their victims often did not. Scholars and students, then, must be careful when reading the awful crimes and deviant practices levelled against minority communities. These documents were both designed to ensure the conviction of individuals and demonize groups which those in authority wanted expelled from their midst by inciting hatred, fear and disgust. The stealing of children, unnatural sexual habits, the poisoning of wells, the bringing of pestilence, the death of livestock or just inviting the anger of God: all of these kinds of charges were common and all were imaginary, despite the number of good, simple souls willing to swear to having witnessed them practised by their neighbours. Beware of such evidence, although again it does provide insight into the minds of people long dead; and this helps us understand their fears, especially the fear of those in some way different from themselves.

6

The Many and Various Forms of Historical Writing

More Recent Categories of Historical Research

Social History

The study of Social History has become one of the most prolific and enriching of the more recent genres of historical research. The study of social structures, the family, marriage, and other vehicles of intimate human and institutional practices is of course very old indeed. Families, dynasties, marriages, and such elements of Social History have always been part of our investigation of previous generations; but the coherently structured analysis of a society and those within it really dates only to the mid-nineteenth century. This followed the rise of the discipline of sociology, reflecting the principles developed in France by Auguste Comte (1798–1857) who sought the almost Newtonian, and certainly Darwinian, 'laws' of society, the way Marx sought the 'laws' that drive history. This social science approach relies greatly on statistics and aggregate evidence that permit modern historians to make generalizations about the social organization of the past beyond individuals or small groups. Large samples, whether based on class, education, location, occupation, religion, or any number of other factors, enabled the social historian to put events into a context that depended very little on individuals or those egregious historical elites that traditional Political History saw as its natural laboratory. Social History is the antithesis to the great man theory or the ancient belief in great and heroic men achieving great things through the exercise of power and

The Experience of History, First Edition. Kenneth Bartlett.

patriotism. In a Social History model everyone contributes, although collectively as part of groups. The contours of history become broad and traditions, practices, laws, and even affinities all are seen as reflections of wider social issues. Of course there are individuals or specific families that emerge as examples of these broader trends; but the proof resides in the larger social picture.

The nature of families thus varies according to the context: was it nuclear or extended? When was the age of marriage for men and women? How were children reared and treated? What was the status of women in both law and custom? Add to these questions an investigation of how and where people lived, how they worked, and how they perceived their status – or how they were perceived by others – and an image of a society can emerge. It is clear that these methods were influenced not only by sociology but also by the somewhat later social science discipline of anthropology. Many historians, especially over the past 30 to 40 years, have used the methods which anthropologists have developed to study very distant and different kinds of society in the present in their investigation of European societies in the past. Particularly influential was the work of the cultural anthropologist Clifford Geertz (1926–2006) whose seminal work in 'symbolic' anthropology revealed how symbols were used to define a society and the roles of people within it. The collective unconscious of a group could be displayed and passed from generation to generation through universally understood symbols and structures that gave shared meaning to a community. His *The Interpretation of Cultures* (1973) had a profound effect on how many social historians then approached the more distant past in Europe, as they argued that in pre-literate or marginally literate societies such symbols and structures had a similar function.

This methodology borrowed from anthropology had a significant impact on social historians as it moved them away from the statistics and numbers of collective experience into something that was much more qualitatively defined, although somewhat more vague. It also brought a rich vein of interdisciplinary study to Social History as now the research of art historians, scholars of literature and religion, folklore and culture had major roles to play. This approach of cultural anthropology has worked better in some areas of historical research than in others, but it has added a powerful new tool for those historians whose interest goes deeply into how men, women, and children in the past understood the world around them, giving students another mechanism for entering the minds of those who lived long ago and saw their world in ways very different from our own.

The second great influence on the development of Social History has been the geographical micro history. In many instances in European studies this method has developed again from the mid-nineteenth century, although in this case not from social science and the desire to find immutable laws but from the Romantic fixation on place and the shared experiences of the community. Many historians in the nineteenth century saw a deep emotional and even irrational association between the individual and the community and the territory it occupied. Nationalism was part of this, but so was Romanticism, sentimentality, and ethics. If we investigate a place, whether a nation like France, or a small village within it, certain elements emerge, such as attachment to the soil and often a simple way of traditional life, a kind of primitive equality – or at least mutual responsibility among classes – a dedication to abstract principles, whether those of the French Revolution or of religion, and, again, a regard for symbols and common practices.

These kinds of Social History have also been extremely useful in understanding communities in the past, explaining why villages of peasants, for example, refused to entertain new farming methods, even though the evidence was clear that their yield would be greater and their wealth increased. It helped explain why some communities adopted the Reformation and others not, why the coming of the railroad was not universally applauded and in some cases violently opposed. Why did some areas remain adamantly republican or royalist, even though the consequences would not be good? These kinds of histories are equally significant in helping us enter the mind of the past. In our modern world we cannot understand why individuals or communities would work against their own best economic or political self-interest or why they would cling to an uncomfortable way of life when they had the opportunity to improve their livelihoods, enjoy greater comfort, see their children better educated and with a chance of even greater advancement.

When these methods were applied in the later nineteenth and early twentieth centuries to the micro histories of area in large European nations, what often emerged was an insight into earlier times, explaining how our concept of progress was not necessarily a positive goal or even a pleasant dream. Remember, when entering that distant country of the past we need all the coordinates possible in our GPS; and we need inoculation against bringing our values and principles with us because things are done differently in that vanished world.

Prosopography

Among groups in the past where evidence tends to be general and institutional rather than specific and individual, a solution to making valid judgments about their experience is prosopography. In its simplest form, prosopography is collective biography, where a community of persons in the past is investigated through their shared characteristics and experiences. Conclusions are made not in the contributions of particular members of this group but on the common elements shared by them all. For example, little can be discovered about the individual monks in a small abbey in rural France in the fourteenth century; but we have important documentation about the lives, activities, habits, expenditures, diets, devotions, practices and charity of the monastic community as a whole. We may have their mortuary records and the entries into its book of novices: these documents together can permit a historian to determine how long the monks lived and whether there were any other correlating factors, such as the quality of diet, the incidence of plague or disease, and the average or mean length of a vocation. These collective observations provide very important insights into that monastic community, the lives of its inhabitants, and its relationship to the outside world.

Another example might be the records of an English Midlands cotton factory at the end of the eighteenth century. Those who toiled in the factory are in many ways anonymous; but we know their names, perhaps their ages, their wages, their tasks in the factory, and when they ceased to be employed. Here, too, the collective biographies of the workers can reveal a great deal about the lives of factory workers in the early years of the Industrial Revolution: what age they began work, whether other family members were employed, as evidenced by common surnames, their wages and jobs, and when they either died or were too old to work. We can determine if wages improved over time and whether these reflected more experience, working longer hours or accomplishing tasks of greater complexity. We can make a judgment on the proportion of men to women and whether their sex determined their tasks and affected their wages. We can assess the effects of illness, especially visitations of 'factory fever' on the workforce and mortality of workers. And, we can correlate this evidence with what we know about the general circumstances in the region, the industry, and even the nation. Did the factory dismiss workers during hard economic times or reduce wages? What effect did competition, availability of raw materials, or better transportation have on the factory employees? In other words, as with the monastery, we can use the collective biographies of people in the past who left little mark on their world to provide extremely useful and important information about them and others like them.

Finally, prosopography can work equally well even when there is only a single piece of evidence. Imagine that a parish register from an English village has been preserved. That single document will record the births, marriages, baptisms, and burials of almost everyone in the community, often over a lengthy period of time (they were legally required to be kept after 1538). From this we can assess the fertility rates in the village, age of first marriage and incidence of second marriages, the age at death, and the toll of child mortality. Otherwise difficult to determine elements of Social History emerge from such records, including the degree of endogamous marriage, that is, how many members of that parish married other members of the parish and how many married outside the local community. This can permit us to make important judgments on the nature of marriage itself, such as those with the most property were most likely to marry outside the locality (technically called exogamous unions). Similarly, prosopography from this single source yields invaluable insights into demographic shifts resulting from external factors, for example, enclosures, factory building nearby or the need for soldiers in time of war.

Gendered Histories

From the moment that Women's History became a powerful subdiscipline among historians, the idea of seeing the past as 'gendered' emerged, although this genre developed somewhat later in its fullest manifestation. So, it is important to begin with Women's History and its close ideological cousin, Feminist History.

Women's History

The idea of investigating the experience of women in the past, rather than simply incorporating them into their usually male dominated societies, arose mostly after the Second World War. This narrative, however, resulted from the various earlier movements agitating for women's individual and collective rights, such as the right to vote, seek an education, hold public office, control their own finances, divorce, and enjoy equal access to employment, among many others. The idea, then, of researching and discussing the past from the perspective of the women was born and the effects have been quite remarkable. Previously, the writing of history had been characterized almost exclusively by a 'male gaze', that is, the perspective of men and the experience and attitudes of men. Women, if they were discussed at all, were seen as male adjuncts, such as wives, mothers, daughters, or mistresses. Their stories were completely bound up in the ambitions and world view of the men around them, with little time spent on their very different experience. It was a man's world, with Political and Military History dominant – the arena of men – reinforced by Economic History and Institutional History equally controlled by men. Only if a woman enjoyed power in a man's world was she given a deep and penetrating study; and these women tended to be unique examples, such as female rulers or outstanding individuals who succeeded in a particular occupation, despite the barriers erected against their ambitions. No one could argue that Queen Elizabeth I (*d.* 1603), Lucrezia Borgia (*d.* 1519), St Teresa of Ávila (*d.* 1582), or Catherine the Great of Russia (*d.* 1796) were ordinary representatives of their sex.

The idea of Women's History arose with the recognition that women had their own voices and these were quite different from the voices of men. The lives of girls and women needed to be investigated on their own terms, using evidence that spoke to their experience: the documents written by men, or even the official evidence of the state, the law, and the church, could not be trusted to reveal the lives of women. This recognition led to a dramatic increase in the use of non-traditional forms of evidence, such as personal letters, diaries, and various documents of Social History, like marriage and dowry contracts, wills and household inventories. General statistical evidence, such as tax, census, and parish documents were revisited to reveal the personal and collective experience and position of women in the family, the community, and the life of the nation. The result has been a remarkable insight into the past and a much richer and more complete knowledge of how those who lived long ago lived their lives. And, now, the lives of all those inhabitants of the past emerged, because women took their places in the social and economic structure. Until very recently the experience of men and women could not be assessed in the same ways, because of the social, legal, and religious restrictions imposed upon females; but the reality of their lives could be analysed on their own terms, giving voice to that half of humanity that was too often silent and invisible in a world dominated by men.

Feminist History

The growing interest in the roles of women and the explosion of women's movements over the past 60 years has created the ideological perspective of Feminist History. This is not just the history of women: it is history in general investigated through a female lens. Events, laws, practices, beliefs, and every other aspect of researching history must be re-evaluated by rejecting the received wisdom of the past and rewriting it from the viewpoint of women. The assumption is that older histories, and most historical evidence, are flawed and indeed unreliable because they were written by men and thus are informed by male attitudes and expectations, whether consciously or subconsciously. Their conclusions, use of evidence, and basic assumptions are misleading because they record the world of men.

Feminist History, then, is by its very nature provocative to a great many historians, mostly older and mostly male, but not exclusively. The ideological platform of feminism becomes the instrument used to dissect the past and this, some argue, limits the historian's ability to draw balanced and fair conclusions, the same kinds of arguments used against Marxist historiography, for example. Critics suggest that any ideological prism distorts the colours of the past and leads to self-serving if not tautological conclusions. Although I agree that any ideologically-based history needs to be used carefully, these accusations are not in fact valid; if they were they would have to apply equally to histories written by men until perhaps the 1960s, as male values constituted their ideological platform. What I suggest is that same advice provided in my discussion of historians in general: never rely on just one book, one historian, or one perspective. Read broadly and use the important and invaluable insights offered by feminist historians as correctives and elaborations for standard histories. Shifting the 'gaze' and reinterpreting evidence from a radically different perspective will lead to a more sophisticated and subtle understanding of the past. Feminist History – with a very few exceptions – is not an ideological assault on traditional male studies, nor a vituperation against patriarchal oppression; rather, it is seeing the experience of the past through a different lens and that is always useful.

Gender History

A further recent elaboration on elements of Social History that conforms not just to traditional or feminist perspectives is the idea of gender. The argument is that men and women at all times – including the past – were formed by influences that defined what it meant to be male or female – or neither. Social roles were 'gendered' by prevailing norms, practices, expectations, religion, and the law. Wife, mother, husband, father: these are the obvious examples of gendered roles, as they were defined until extremely recently by sex and sexual identity and function. But, what did it mean to be male? How is masculinity defined? How were the lives of men in the past conditioned by a set of expectations? The same, of course, applies to women. Gender historians argue that individuals were certainly given a set of roles to play but that each individual struggled to find a degree of integrity and self-awareness within these roles, or reject them altogether and seek a personal definition of themselves. This tension between the complex social codes built into any society's concept of gender roles and the reality of each individual's experience has resulted in a very significant insight into how a community conditioned its members and how individuals fitted or did not fit into that community.

Some examples should help. In the past European men were often defined according to the elements of their social status and these were powerfully infused with concepts of gender. Nobles were expected to be warriors, to fight and duel to defend their socially constructed sense of honour; they hunted and used weapons; they were promiscuous lovers, while sustaining a primary affection for one woman; they had social accomplishments which they wore lightly, whether skill in music, dance, or poetry; they were pious enough to sustain the established religion; and they were wise and educated enough to offer advice to their prince or to the councils of the republic. These, however, are all socially conditioned. Well-born young men were trained to achieve these goals and learnt to practise them in public and in private: it was expected of them. But how many men found these expectations unrealistic or even uncongenial? What happened to those who refused to play their roles and chose instead to actualize their individuality in other ways?

The same can be said of women. The model of the modest, chaste, obedient, pious and dutiful daughter, wife and mother was everywhere in Europe until the nineteenth century. Women were reared to meet these expectations; their education was limited and their duty was to submit their characters to the wills of the men around them. They had few rights and fewer options than men to escape the narrow lives prescribed for them. Some managed to define themselves in their own terms and thrive; but these were usually privileged women. Too often the gender expectations for women and girls left them with little alternative than to suffer and obey.

Gender History, then, is really an element of Social History but it is also an extremely subtle interdisciplinary reading of the past. Trying to understand how gendered social expectations were inculcated and how flexible these might have been are difficult areas of investigation, because getting at the reality of the inner lives of people long dead is a challenge, especially if many of these were women who could not easily rebel against social norms and seldom left evidence if they did or even wished to try. Still, we learn a great deal about a society by studying both the general expectations imposed on its members and from the evidence of those who could not or refused to conform. We all, even today, live gendered lives, so investigating the role of gender in the past is instructive and important.

Queer History

Of all groups ostracized from their European societies, gays and lesbians were among the most inhumanely treated. Biblical injunctions, religious teaching, legal proscriptions, and social rejection characterized those who practised same-sex relationships. Indeed, the term 'queer' was once seriously pejorative; but recently it has been reclaimed as a mark of pride in a community that had been marginalized and silenced for much of history. However, as part of the agitation for greater and protected individual rights and dignity and the freedom movements that animated the 1960s up to the present, lesbian, gay, bisexual and transgendered people have secured widespread recognition as full members of society, including in a great many western nations the legal right to marry. With this new openness and pride in their community, a growing interest in the history of queer activity naturally developed. Like Women's History, these rigorous studies have given what had been until so recently silenced voices a forum to speak and witness for their experience. And, this has been a good thing, inasmuch as until just a few decades ago the history of gays, lesbians and transgendered people had been left either to amateurs who often lacked the formal training to discover and use evidence correctly or to those conservative authors who wrote against homosexuality from a religious or prejudiced perspective.

The researching and analysis of material on the gays and lesbians of the past is a difficult task. Because their affections and practices were illegal and punishable by the most terrible sanctions, including castration and burning, few admitted to their sexuality. Indeed, most of the evidence comes from the prosecution of what was called sodomy. Nevertheless, the transcripts of these trials are often of the greatest interest and use because they reveal much about the communities persecuted under the law. All ranks and occupations were found, including priests and nuns; male prostitutes appear, occasionally dressed as women, something that the celebrated prostitutes of Venice complained about on many occasions, as it led to the loss of clients. The practice of sodomy itself was described on many occasions, and the prosecution of men who sodomized women appeared together with male couples, as both had contravened the same law against 'unnatural' intercourse.

Oddly, lesbianism was not universally illegal, and consequently there are fewer instances of same-sex female love in court documents. Still, evidence does emerge in bishops' or archdeacons' visitations of convents and in petitions for annulment. Again, students and scholars must know where to look for exemplary material relevant to surreptitious practices carried out in secret by men and women who usually went to great lengths to conceal their true natures out of fear of socially imposed shame or terrible legal punishments.

There are collateral pieces of evidence that indicate how widespread the practice of homosexuality was believed to have been. In Renaissance Florence, for example, laws for the establishment of official brothels licensed by the republic were justified by the need to make women available to unmarried men to protect them from homosexuality. Documents presented for the annulment of marriages sometimes give a husband's homosexuality as the reason the union was not consummated and hence invalid. Occasionally, lesbian tendencies by wives will appear as well. But, it is in the personal evidence of individuals that some of the more interesting material is found. Private letters between men, poetry written to same-sex lovers, medical treatises and church documents can provide insight into the minds and lives of these clandestine communities. What every historian must be wary of, however, are the literary or social conventions of the time. Men often spoke of their love of one another, but it was not of the active kind. References to ancient Greek culture might imply same-sex interest; it also just might be a classical literary allusion. Close male friends were far more physically demonstrative of their friendship than we are today; but that does not mean sexual interest. And, until quite recent times, everyone shared their beds with others, regardless of status. To have evidence that two men slept together does not necessarily mean at all that they engaged in sex.

Still, this very new genre of historical investigation has brought into view the lives of men and women long sentenced to silence and the dark corners of history. And, as the sub-discipline matures and reaches ever more deeply into the social worlds of the past a greater understanding of our LGBTQ ancestors will emerge and this will add greater insights into our shared past.

Children's History

With the publication over the past half century of books dealing with the history of children and childhood, another complex element has been added to our understanding of the societies of the past. What did it mean to be young in a world that did not necessarily see that stage of life as a separate experience? Childhood and adolescence, in fact, are quite modern concepts. For most people at most times children were merely immature or not yet fully developed adults. They were not released from hard, physical labour from a very young age, if born poor, for example. Children as young as five were sent to work in the fields, mines, or factories and up until that time they were often seen as a danger to the family's position, as the boy or girl was another mouth to feed. Children of a higher status were recognized as important, as boys carried on the family name, had an opportunity to add to the wealth of the family through success in business, war, the church, or politics; or, a young man of elite status could marry well and acquire a large dowry that would be at his disposal. Girls, however, posed the problem of having to have a dowry, and the amount would be determined by and seen as reflecting the social status of the extended kin. Girls were expensive, and many of them ended up in convents, some at an early age when they really could not fully understand the commitment they were forced to make.

Although boys and girls did not mature as quickly as those today, girls were married younger and boys often older. Thus, definitions of childhood or even adolescence are hard to make. If an elite girl is professed as a novice to a convent at the age of eight, has she ceased to be a child? If married at fourteen? If a mother at fifteen? These are the kinds of questions a historian of childhood needs to address.

Elite children were often seen as miniature adults, dressed like their parents and depicted in poses quite inappropriate to their ages – at least from our perspective. The terrible toll of childhood mortality made deep affective relationships between parents and children unwise; but does that mean that the kind of affection we assume parents had for their children was lacking or different? Childhood education was discussed in every generation because the nurturing of the young would bear fruit in the engaged citizen if male and a dutiful wife and mother if female. Authors who wrote about children tended to repeat these kinds of moral platitudes and offer advice that seems very conventional and uninteresting. But we need, again, to look at the evidence of Children's History to discover things about the history of the family and the fundamental values the ambient social world held dear. Why, for example, did elite women begin to breastfeed their own children by the end of the eighteenth century rather than rely on wet-nurses? Was it the result of the Enlightenment, the writings the Romantics, or Jean-Jacques Rousseau? Was a different role for children in the family emerging as a consequence of a great many factors that saw children not as miniature adults but as pure and innocent creatures in need of protection and their own culture? Regardless, these changes only applied to the elite and soon after the middle class: the poor continued to use their children as labour from the earliest age possible, with little concern for purity or innocence. It would take the intervention of the state to change that.

Consequently, the history of children, besides being an important sub-genre of Social History, is worth researching because of the insights attitudes towards children reveal. The changing nature of educational tools and curricula, the increase in the number of books written for and about children and parenting and the change in the nature of the bourgeois family, with its sentimental view of childhood, all indicate substantial social change which can be seen as the outward and visible signs of very different economic, cultural, and even political values. Children's History is a very interdisciplinary interest and one which has proved its merit as a distinct category, separate from, but closely associated with, Social History.

Transnational History

An element of World History is Transnational History: that is, historical research that reaches across national or political borders to assess general questions not limited by a single political unit. This genre of history has become very important in recent years, driven by our recognition that political borders are almost always artificial. This is especially true in Africa, the Indian subcontinent, and the Middle East, where political boundaries were set by imperial powers in the nineteenth century with little or no consideration for the reality of geographical, tribal or religious affiliations or enmities long present before Europeans imposed their divisions on entire continents. States carved out of the former Ottoman Empire after the First World War had more to do with which European powers were to be rewarded with the spoils of the vanquished, in this case Turkey, an ally of Imperial Germany.

Hostilities between Sunni and Shia Muslims meant little to those European mapmakers, for example, and economic viability was not sufficiently recognized; and European protectorates protected mostly European interests. Similarly, in the partition of what was British India in 1947, the question of religion was naturally paramount, with Muslim Pakistan separated from Hindu India, despite the obvious reality that millions of Hindus were left in Pakistan and Muslims in India. Borders were – and remain – dangerous points of contention; and the Pakistani civil war that resulted in the creation of Bangladesh in 1971 revealed just how flawed this partition was. Even in Europe, the creation or re-creation of new states from the composite, multinational empires of Austria-Hungary, Germany, and Russia caused an instability and ethnic tension that erupted into another world war. Today, the disintegration of the Soviet Union has created an equally unstable situation among several of the formerly constituent parts of the Soviet Empire.

Transnational History, then, looks at issues without the straitjacket of national borders, as these have been revealed as artificial, even makeshift. The migrations of people, especially after the partition of India and the relocation of millions of displaced persons after the Second World War provided evidence that history sometimes is best studied outside the nation state.

Diaspora Studies

An aspect of this transnational category of history is Diaspora Studies. We usually associate the term with the Jews, beginning with the campaigns of Titus in 70 AD in Palestine. Jews spread across the entire world as it was then known, reaching every nation in Europe, Africa, and even China. To study the Jewish people, then, is to look beyond borders into how a group seen as 'other' managed to thrive and build cultures in their host nations, despite constant persecution and legal restrictions. A similar story could be told of the Roma people, or, as they are commonly known, gypsies. (The term is a corruption of Egyptians, as this was erroneously believed to have been the origin of the Roma.) From their original homeland in India, they lived nomadic lives, crossing every national border in Europe and beyond, again despite regular persecutions. They, too, were in nations but not of those nations. If the Jews were not permitted to enter Christian political, social, or in some places economic life, the Roma chose not to, existing on the margins of society. In this example, as well, a history of the Roma would by definition be transnational and conform to the principles of Diaspora.

Other examples should indicate the importance of writing and studying history from a perspective that has little to do with the nation state. The expulsion of the Jews and Muslims from Spain in 1492 resulted in diasporas. To learn about these communities and their success in finding new homes elsewhere in the world presupposes a method that is transnational. Evidence must be found in many places and in many diverse kinds of records. From Venice to Istanbul to North Africa, these expelled Spaniards – Jewish and Muslim – built new communities and lives elsewhere. They once constituted a relatively clearly defined group in a specific place, the Iberian Peninsula; however, after 1492 they were without a homeland, although they could not help but carry the traditions of Iberian life with them wherever they went. Peoples forced or who choose to abandon their traditional homelands might be stateless but they are not rootless. The memories of what they left behind, their language, names, and traditions were inextricably connected with the places they left and would consequently influence their new homes for a long period of time. These connections and memories are important in the history of any people, so Transnational History – or Diaspora Studies – is an efficacious and helpful addition to the arsenal of historical perspectives.

Holocaust Studies

I am separating out a huge area of modern historical research on the Jews and those around them because of the monstrosity of the crime. The murder of 6 million Jews by the Nazis and their collaborators during the Second World War has given rise to an industry of historical research. This is largely because it is so difficult to comprehend how such a thing was possible so recently in a continent which had been host to Jews from the time of the destruction of the temple. Later generations had this need to know how and why such a thing could occur and to witness for the dead and dispossessed and to understand as far as it is possible the motives and actions of the perpetrators. The Nazis helped build this industry through their meticulous records: we know a great deal about this stain on the soul of the human family, details that describe what happened and under whose orders. But the compelling desire to know why is different. This can never be determined with absolute certainty because we are studying the actions and institutions of entire nations and hundreds of thousands of often ordinary men and women who committed unspeakable acts. What matters here, however, is that story continues to be told, researched, and revealed. The Holocaust as a moment in history is unique in its horror and hence will always be a magnetic subject for research and writing, even if we concede that no single satisfactory explanation will ever be given.

Genocide Studies

More recently, other national, religious or ethnic groups have appropriated or paralleled the title of Holocaust or absorbed the term and the Jewish experience under the Nazis into a broader category of Genocide Studies. The point is to bring historical and legal attention to the sufferings of other groups and to establish a pattern of behaviour that both preceded and followed the Nazi attempt to exterminate the Jews. The Armenian community has vigorously argued that the Turkish slaughter of millions of Armenians in 1915 constituted the first modern exercise of a policy of genocide. Subsequently, Ukrainians point to the artificial famine in their nation ordered by Josef Stalin in 1932–1933, the Holodomor, as a policy of genocide. And there were massacres in Rwanda in 1994 where one tribal group (Hutus) slaughtered as many as three-quarters of the rival Tutsis, as well as many thousands of Hutus who opposed the policy.

Closely associated with this is the policy of ethnic cleansing. This sad practice of attempting to make a geographical area the territory of one national or religious group by killing or expelling others in that territory not of that group has a long and terrible history. Some of this can be assigned to Jewish History, as Jews were often the victims of such practices, including their expulsion from England by Edward I in 1290 or the expulsion of Jews and Moors from Spain in 1492. Many instances of such ethnic cleansing occurred throughout the world, including North America, where French Acadians were driven from Canada to Louisiana in the eighteenth century after the Seven Years' War, and where thousands of aboriginal tribes were driven from their lands and onto reserves. Most recently, the terrible instances of such barbaric policies in the Balkans following the disintegration of Yugoslavia in the 1990s reinforced in the modern historical record how prevalent certain inexcusable actions remain, reinforcing the brief against Whig History.

World History

Since the 1980s there has been an expansion of the genres of historical research and writing to facilitate a different way of investigating the past. Of these one of the most effective and popular is World History. World History has as its area of interest the entire globe and seeks to establish patterns among the peoples and states of the world that can elucidate elements of shared experience or help explain fundamental differences. The method is not comparative, that is, it does not choose just a few examples of a certain historical pattern and analyse it from evidence in just two or three places; rather, it attempts to discuss these elements everywhere they arise or, on the contrary where they fail to appear. The advantage is that new insights and understanding can be obtained by looking at similar issues in many different contexts. An example might be how feudal structures of landholding and elite power manifested itself in places as diverse as Europe and Japan; or, how an institution such as slavery was practised virtually everywhere around the world. As a result of this methodology, World History is usually studied and taught thematically, with particular areas of interests reviewed globally, even at different times. Chronology remains an important consideration, but the thematic structures under investigation provide the essential organizing principle and evidence from different times is compared to different places.

World History often implies an element of anthropology. What are the common structures in human societies that are similar or different and why? When approaching non-western civilizations, an anthropological approach is useful because it helps overcome the natural bias of 'western centricity'. Western civilization is what we know and we understand it viscerally; we are programmed by its contours and we are guided by its assumptions. Anthropologists have had to overcome this western lens in order to study other cultures on their own terms, and this method can be useful to students of World History.

Big History

This is the most recent and the most ambitious of all of the categories of historical research. In the 1990s, the idea emerged that human civilization was but a small and inappropriately privileged moment in the evolution of the universe. With the advent of space travel, powerful interstellar telescopes, and advances in the sciences of biology, physics, and chemistry, it would be more generous, it was argued, to place the advent and supremacy of humans on earth in a much broader context. An American professor working in Australia, David Christian (b. 1946), called this 'Big History', and a new genre of research was born, although not without a degree of controversy.

In its simplest form, Big History starts with the creation of the universe, the Big Bang, and consequently covers the approximately 14 billion years since that formative event. The earliest period of research is really then driven by astronomy, with the development of stars and galaxies, and only afterwards any special position allotted to life on earth. Even here, however, human civilization is not interpreted as the conclusion of this evolutionary process: the teleology of the universe has nothing to do with human supremacy. If anything, that is a biological accident and of little significance. How can the past 5000 years of standard human history compete with the 14 billion years of the existence of the universe? Human history in reality is seen as part of a biological process of evolution that traces how living things developed, mutated, and grew ever more complex until humanoid creatures began walking upright and migrated out of Africa. In this historical vision, anthropology is as important as recorded or archaeological history. The ability to control and use fire, the formation of tribal groups, the establishment of settled agriculture and the domestication of animals all take precedence over the invention of writing or the construction of the pyramids. Indeed, the usual categories of history – those discussed above almost without exception – are reassigned to footnotes in the larger story of the universe and the place of the earth and human habitation on our home planet.

A true advocate of Big History will argue that knowledge of astronomy, cosmology, physics, chemistry, biology, anthropology and mathematical demographics are much more useful in explaining where we are and how we got here. The traditional discussions of history as distinct periods of the past evaporate, and established areas of research like the ancient world, the Middle Ages, and the Enlightenment are only short paragraphs in a much longer story. What matters, as in World History, to which it can in some small ways be compared, at least on earth, are themes, parallel developments, and the effects of natural conditions and extreme events on the human story. These themes, it is suggested, place mankind back where we belong as servants rather than masters of the universe and the forces of nature.

There have been many critics of this sub-discipline, of course. Some note that very few scholars or students can master the many scientific disciplines needed to draw reliable conclusions about Big History. Others say it is in fact a reversion to an almost medieval view of the pre-eminent role of distant, abstract forces in human affairs, reducing the defining power of human intelligence, free will, and culture to insignificance. Replace, they observed, these huge cosmological forces with the word God and the divine teleology of medieval and early religious historians comes back to life after centuries of sleep in their coffins following the Enlightenment. Nevertheless, despite such objections, Big History has found a receptive audience. Not surprisingly, those who are committed to the ecological movement and proselytize for the immediate threats of climate change see a powerful and persuasive ally in Big History. As a result this approach has become more ideological than it needed to have been; but, as I have often said, that is one of the central values of seeing history as not only charting change over time but contributing to that change by seeing different patterns, objectives, and methods in our continuous search for an answer to the question of who we are and how we got here.

7

The Writing of History

We have already discussed the forms of history, the categories into which it can be divided, and the need for and careful use of evidence. Now, we need to investigate the writing of history itself, how it changed over time, how historical texts use evidence to reach reasonable conclusions, and how an effective argument can be crafted using both evidence and persuasive prose.

Whether history is written by a senior scholar, celebrated in her or his field, or by a student trying to develop a convincing thesis for an undergraduate paper, the process is essentially the same. The differences reside in the sophistication of the analysis and the nature of the evidence, as well as in a much more complex relationship between the professional historian and his or her audience. Regardless who is writing history, all evidence must be carefully selected and tested as to its reliability; every sentence needs to contribute to the argument and be effectively crafted; every paragraph must reinforce the intention of the author; and the entire section, chapter or paper must be coherent and engaging: tedious and boring prose can give any subject a bad reputation. What this means is that the idiot who stated that history is nothing more than one damn thing after another never read history because that is exactly what the discipline is not. (The quote has been attributed to a great many people from the historian Arnold Toynbee (*d.* 1975) to Henry Ford.) Evidence – or facts or things – have little significance in themselves: everything depends on how these are used

The Experience of History, First Edition. Kenneth Bartlett.

to elucidate the experience of the past. The accumulation of evidence for its own sake is at best a kind of curious but sterile antiquarianism; it is not unlike someone who memorizes a huge collection of baseball statistics but has never watched a game or understands how it is played.

The Writing of History in the Past

What all of this means is that there remains – and appropriately so – much of the classical and Renaissance belief that history and rhetoric are closely connected. Indeed, the point is not only to reveal some aspect of the past but also to convince the reader of its importance; and this requires stylistic polish and rhetorical skill. Organization is an absolute: the argument must be logical and unfold organically from the evidence. There needs to be a discursive response to likely challenges to your interpretation of evidence and a critical assessment of received scholarship on the subject. This will often include an elaboration on or rejection of other historical studies both to validate your own research and conclusions and to show where another's might be less than convincing or inadequate. It also presupposes a methodology of your own, the structure used to reveal the process of change over time. These are all fundamental elements of persuasion, the art of rhetoric, reflecting both the theoretical and expository aspects of the historian's craft. To believe for a moment that facts speak for themselves is a failure to admit to the historian's role in marshalling and using those 'facts', as well as a naïve belief that facts have a voice. The voice, as I have said, is that of the historian; so, the facts do not speak for themselves: the historian speaks for them and to a degree through them.

The Deeds of Great Men

Because ancient and early modern historians saw history as the record of the deeds of great men which could serve as examples for others and to impart moral lessons and reinforce patriotism, their histories were often structured as biographies or as narratives of events in which an individual or a major event, like a war, provided the glue to hold the story together. Evidence was used to illustrate the virtues and power of these men and was often subordinated to the service of the theme of the righteousness of a particular cause and the remarkable attributes of the heroes of these narratives. These were very much stories, narratives full of rhetorical invention to ensure that the message would be clearly received. The enemies of these historical heroes were painted as worse than evil and their intentions wicked, while the ability of heroic individuals to control the sequence of events was almost superhuman. There was little or no attempt at balance, and evidence was consequently used in a very partisan manner. Material that seemed to challenge the good intentions and virtues of the great man in control of events was suppressed, as was any consideration of the positive characteristics of his enemies. These are the stories of the fall of princes, of hubris, and of fatal flaws. The structures and traditions of drama and literature infected history to the point that it seemed to be almost a genre of literature.

History as a Divine Plan

The institutionalization of Christianity altered this to a degree by superimposing a divine teleology. Events unfolded as they did because God's plan was being worked out through the actions of men – and occasionally women. Evidence suffered even more, as it was seen not as the record of human events but of divine intention. And, the image of power changed, with humble, poor, persecuted martyrs showing they had more influence and certainly greater virtue than the Roman emperors who were condemning them: spiritual constancy and divine approbation were now the ideal models to emulate. In this medieval version of history, belief superseded evidence and divine intervention becomes the real cause of events and the prime mover of change. Despite the return to the ancient model of literary, rhetorical historiography in the Italian Renaissance in the fifteenth century, the Reformation of the sixteenth resulted in a reversion to a confessional form of historical writing. The Reformation – in whatever form and whatever place in Europe it occurred – had to prove that it was a signal model of divine intervention and a revolution in the original sense of the term, that is, a revolving back to the original, better, and more orthodox circumstances of church and society which had been sullied by impure, indeed demonic, accretions. The reform inherent in the movement was the reinterpretation of the past to show how humanity had been led astray by human imperfection and a reformation was needed to bring it back to the simple guidelines that God had provided for salvation. History was essential to this process, as it had to show how the way was lost and how it was now recovered. History, then, became the story of the return to the purity and virtues of the apostolic church, illuminated only by divine texts and not subject to the imperfect and sinful influence of imperfect men.

The Scientific Revolution, The Enlightenment, and the 'Laws' of History

It was with the Scientific Revolution and Enlightenment that this form of historical writing which attempted to resolve the ways of God with human action was largely rejected in favour of human causality. This method sees change over time occurring because of the actions of men and women, all of which have consequences which become the engines of historical change. This way of writing history was powerfully influenced by the Scientific Revolution's belief that the laws of nature were at last being revealed and codified. History was seen not unlike Newton's laws of physics where cause and effect were interpreted almost mechanistically. Discover the laws that govern history – or human society – and an instrument for the understanding of change in human affairs can emerge, meaning that events in the future might not be foretold in any specific detail, but that the general direction of human progress can at least be imagined. Similarly, if these laws of history can be harnessed, then change can be directed towards certain goals which could make human society and its institutions fairer, better, and more in tune with a beneficent nature.

During the nineteenth century a belief in the need to define the laws of history and human society became widely accepted. Thinkers such as Auguste Comte (*d.* 1857) argued that the laws of society can be discovered and if known then manipulated (Positivism); he consequently invented sociology. And, the belief that political action itself had clearly discernible forces driving it gave rise to political science, that is, the science of politics. Similarly, in Adam Smith's 1776 *The Wealth of Nations*, the forces driving economics, such as supply and demand, enlightened self-interest, with its unseen hand of the marketplace, become almost as mechanistic as Newton's laws themselves. This desire to discover the laws of history and the laws of society, politics, and economics produced in fact very positive results, as the collecting of statistics in a great many areas and the charting of large movements of populations and other demographic evidence were adopted as the data needed to define those laws. Political and economic documents were investigated more carefully to uncover their deeper significance and how they revealed the operation of those 'laws'. Consequently, the evidence available for writers of history became much richer.

Karl Marx (*d.* 1883) was the most emphatic believer in the laws of history, largely because he truly believed that he had discovered them. Working from his contention that economic forces were the motives for class identification and conflict, Marx argued that historical change developed from purely material considerations. He adapted the dialectical structure of the historian and philosopher Georg Hegel (1770–1831) to propose his theory of dialectical materialism which became the instrument for projecting the inevitability of revolution and the final victory of socialism. Marxist historiography is a highly mechanistic model and very much a reflection of that nineteenth-century acceptance of the reality of historical, social, economic, or political laws, permitting the future to become visible. History, then, not only recorded the past and interpreted the present but also provided the material for seeing the future. This permitted the American journalist, Lincoln Steffens (*d.* 1936), to remark after a visit to the Soviet Union in 1919 that he 'had the seen the future and it works'.

History and Social Darwinism

Another writer who affected the writing of history in the past was Charles Darwin (*d.* 1882), whose *On the Origin of Species* appeared in 1859. In this book on natural history, that is biological science, Darwin finally removed God or any other supernatural force from science or from the writing of human history. Natural selection, which operates as a law of nature, was the driving force of evolutionary change which required entire species to evolve over time to survive and adapt to a new environment. A great many observers noted that, although Darwin's examples all came from animals, like birds and dogs, he set the course for human evolution as well. Humanity, after all, was part of nature and men and women were animals in that kingdom, so we are governed by those same laws. Darwin himself recognized this when he published in 1871 *The Descent of Man*. When Darwin's continuators and supporters applied these ideas from biology to the human condition and history, they introduced terms like 'the survival of the fittest', indicating that human beings change as well over time with their environment.

These ideas had a powerful effect on how political, social, economic, and military decisions were taken in the later nineteenth and first half of the twentieth centuries. Concepts of race, in which some are 'favoured' over others, exploded in European thought, and history began to reflect the need for those favoured races to challenge others in a dangerous zero sum game in which the fittest will survive and the weaker examples face extinction or subjection. In society, the poor were poor because of their inability to compete; the same was true in economics and business: it was pointless, indeed invidious, to attempt to change this situation because it was a law of nature. The weak will languish and the strong will thrive. In an age when Europeans were dividing the world among themselves through conquest, colonization, and international business expansion, these ideas justified imperialism, the subjection of other peoples and even the repulsive concept of human slavery. Whoever was strong enough to force his will on others was part of the necessary process of evolution, moving humanity along the road to greater adaptation and success. Thus, whatever succeeded was right, leaving the weak, the sick, the infirm – or the merely technologically underdeveloped – to accept subjugation by favoured, superior populations.

It was the duty of history to record these successes and failures so that others could learn from them and recognize the undeniable and clearly manifest verdicts of science. These histories, then, saw evidence as very much the narrative of the victors and a vindication of the strong and decisive, even ruthless. A new kind of teleology infected such historical writing: the celebration of success and the vilification of weakness. Evidence was often without nuance, as the results were the critical conclusion, not the process. Colonized peoples were infantilized or described in patronizing or derogatory terms, because the path to realizing the fruits of human evolution resided with the imperialists and the victors. It could often be reduced to the simple dictum of whatever is, is right. This was the new law of history.

Writing History after the Second World War

Exploding this self-serving ideology required the unspeakable acts of the Nazi regime in Germany (1933–1945), with its racial theories, absurd belief in supermen, and the consequent need to liquidate those 'unfavoured' races that stood in their way: Jews, Gypsies, the weak and infirm and many others. These terrible events, together with the dismantling of empires, and the decline of Europe after the Second World War, led to a re-examination of the role that history played both in reinforcing some of the pernicious ideas that had led to the holocaust and war and in sustaining what amounted to elite, hierarchical structures so often present in the historical canon. The military and economic pre-eminence of the United States after the war stimulated new genres of historical research – such as those discussed in the previous chapter – because a new world order had obviously emerged and it had to be explained.

The Cold War might have restricted the freedom of historians on both sides of that divide to challenge certain officially sanctioned positions, but this in itself drove many to look into other narratives of other groups, many of whom had been largely silent. Finally, the enormous expansion of higher education after the Second World War meant that more historians were writing more history from more points of view and with different forms of evidence. This very profusion of historical research caused a tidal wave of new approaches by men and women less bound to a traditional methodology or system and eager to carve out new territories of knowledge. Protected by academic tenure, supported by granting systems that provided funds for new forms of research, and galvanized by the profound social changes of the 1960s and 1970s, these historians, many of them young themselves, re-energized our discipline, providing powerful voices and rigorous evidence for fundamental change. As I have often said, history is the study of historians and it is not an accident that so many of the new areas of research emerged after the war and that so many previously difficult subjects from race to sexuality found advocates anxious to see how the world changed over time, especially as that change had been so rapid and so dramatic; and for the first time all of the inhabitants of the past were recognized as meriting study, including those whose voices had been consciously suppressed.

The Writing of History Today

This brief overview of the development of historiography was necessary to indicate that historians work within the paradigm of their own times and write histories that speak to the issues that dominate their intellectual, cultural, social, political, and economic worlds. What we need to do now is to look at how this is done. What, exactly do historians do and how do they do it?

The most obvious place to begin is at the beginning: what motivates a historian to investigate a particular moment of the past? In the case of students, this question seldom arises, as the usual motivation for their work is fulfilling the requirements of their instructors and earning academic credit; however, even here, there is often room for choosing or at least refining an area of research to reflect personal interests or pure curiosity. So, let's assume, then, that historical research – as with all significant research – is curiosity driven: the desire to know more about something and understand both its contribution to historical change and its relevance to the present discourse on the subject. Thus, the first element in writing history is to recognize that there is something about the past that you, the historian, and your contemporaries do not know; or, that the received scholarship on a specific issue is no longer satisfying to modern readers. The spark for this burst of curiosity, then, might be the discovery of new evidence, or the need to reinterpret old evidence in light of later events or perspectives. Knowledge in every discipline, but particularly history, must be constantly revisited to assess its validity to every generation: as the world changes, so does history.

An Example

Once that spark of curiosity has been struck, the area of research needs to be formulated into a question, because history is written to address questions and postulate answers that satisfy the historian and his or her audience. But, these questions can never be definitively answered, as each historian will suggest what might have happened and why but can never know all of the circumstances surrounding the moment of time in which the event occurred. Let me give you an example: What motivated Lorenzaccio (Lorenzino de'Medici) to murder his cousin Duke Alessandro of Florence in 1537? Despite your uncovering in the library a substantial body of historical scholarship already written on this event, beginning with historians who were living in Florence at the time, you do not feel satisfied that this earlier work resolves the problem. You want another approach or more evidence or a fresh interpretation.

When formulating your question, it becomes increasingly clear how the writing of history itself changes over time. You discover that in the case of Lorenzaccio, contemporary historians who were very close to the duke and his assassin interpreted the event from several perspectives, with little agreement, except for its consequences: the final suppression of the Florentine republic and the establishment of an absolute monarchy under the Medici with the accession of Alessandro's successor, Cosimo I (*r.* 1537–1574). But, the nineteenth century, based conveniently on a self-serving document written later by Lorenzaccio from exile, saw the assassination of the loathsome Duke Alessandro as an act of heroic tyrannicide, reflecting the desire for freedom and justice that characterized much European writing in general in the nineteenth century. The French poet and dramatist Alfred de Musset (1810–1857) even wrote a play, *Lorenzaccio* (1834), in which these principles of Romantic heroism and self-sacrifice in the name of liberty were paramount; but this view had little to do with the reality of the situation in 1537. His audience was liberal Europeans after the July Revolution of 1830 and his intent was to use history as an impetus for change and, if necessary, revolution. Later still, with the rise of the study of psychology and the work of men like Sigmund Freud (1856–1939), Lorenzaccio's actions take on the aura of madness, reflecting the complex, indeed unnatural, relationship between the two cousins;

in this context, Lorenzaccio acted from deep psychological motives of hatred and insanity, with little reference to the political, social, or cultural situation at the time of the murder.

Finally, as I write this, the murder of Alessandro has been viewed through very different modern lenses: race, gender, and sexuality. Duke Alessandro had very pronounced African features: he was the illegitimate child of a Moorish slave in Rome, with Pope Clement VII de'Medici (*r.* 1523–34) possibly his father. Did his race and the circumstances of his birth have any role in his behaviour as duke or in how he has been treated by historians? Similarly, Alessandro and his assassin, Lorenzaccio, were sexually violent predators; in fact, Alessandro was lured to his death by Lorenzaccio with the promise of jointly raping Lorenzaccio's beautiful but chaste sister (or young aunt – the sources vary); and there were rumours of a homosexual relationship between the two cousins.

Framing the Question

What this one example indicates is that identifying a question which on the surface appears straightforward (Why did Lorenzaccio murder Alessandro?) is hardly simple at all. The historian must establish a revisionist position by first taking all of the earlier scholarship and evidence into account; but then that evidence and received scholarship must be revisited and reassessed according to rigorous modern standards. This means not just accepting the evidence used by others but reviewing it, travelling to the state archives in Florence and elsewhere and looking again at the documents and hope to find others which can bring more clarity to the question. When you then address the question yourself, you need to decide how much you intend to take the conclusions of others into account. An event like the murder of Alessandro is complex in itself because it was a secret plan, hatched by a young man with severe psychological problems. Except for the assistance of a professional murderer, he largely acted alone, and his target, Alessandro, brought out strong reactions from those around him, which resulted in their testimony to the event being untrustworthy. The beginning of the historian's task is indeed daunting, but that is what makes it so worthwhile. While we may never determine exactly what happened on that night in 1537 and why, we can understand the environment at the end of the Florentine republic and the foundation of a tyrannical monarchy far better through our research. In other words, the framing of our question about the murder of Alessandro goes well beyond a study of the event itself and deeply into a significant hinge moment of history, when a fundamental change was taking place and the liberty of not only Florence but the entire Italian peninsula was in question. Such is the value of identifying interesting and important historical problems.

The State of the Question

The question has thus been framed. What is now required is for you, the historian, to acquire as much contextual and historiographical knowledge as possible about the question. How this occurs depends to a great degree on what method you intend to employ. What kind of history do you want to write? Every modern work of history requires that there be a 'state of the question' chapter. This follows the story of the problem you wish to pursue from its earliest iteration until the immediate present. Who has written what and when about the problem or similar problems in the past? The value of this is first to indicate that your approach and conclusions will be new and make a contribution to scholarship. Why else would you re-examine the question? Then, it is important to note the inadequacies of earlier studies. Why is a new one needed? Here, you must be precise and comprehensively evaluate what the received literature has concluded by revealing the imperfect use of evidence, or the missing of important documentation, the immaturity of the methodology or its ideological restrictions, the lack of clarity or consistency in the exposition, or the failure to take into account material in other languages or sources from other disciplines. Often this 'state of the question' chapter will appear to be a dialogue with other historians, many distinguished and long dead, others of little consequence but part of the conversation nonetheless.

In this review of the question, tone is very important. To patronize the work of others, to dismiss it flippantly as moronic, underdeveloped, incomprehensible, fundamentally flawed, or worthless is to set yourself up as an omniscient scholar who is about to correct all the misconceptions of the past, recorded in works by mental and methodological inferiors. This is hardly an impression you wish to establish: it is supercilious and unprofessional. Certainly, many previous discussions of your subject will be found wanting and these infelicities should be carefully noted; but the tone should be one of professional engagement, not vain superiority. Finally, be sure that when you criticize the work of others you do not commit the same mistakes yourself. If you observe that certain categories of documentation were not consulted, you must do so and note clearly why this was important. If you rail against a work of history because of its ideological or methodological structure, be sure that you have not just replaced one sterile ideological approach with another. If you expose opaque thinking, lack of coherence, or unsubstantiated generalizations, be sure you have avoided these sins as well: it is hard to accept the authority of a work that repeats the scholarly imperfections reviled in others.

In your review of the research on the subject, be precise about why a new assessment of the question is needed. So, if you complain that earlier research did not investigate a particular set of documents or failed to use a certain archive, say why this is so significant. The world is full of information and any historian must make judicious decisions as to what will be used and how in order to control the vast evidence that survives in so many areas of study. Indicate why an omission has compromised the conclusions of other works or why the question must now be re-evaluated, given the availability of recently discovered or opened repositories. It is not enough to say that recent access to the archives of the Holy Office (Inquisition) in Rome or the records of the former Soviet Union were not available to earlier historians and hence their conclusions are flawed: you must say why these documents are critical and ideally which ones will alter the results of earlier research.

Deciding on a Beginning and an End

The next item usually found in the introductory chapter or chapters is where your work fits into the overall trajectory of your subject. This is the necessary response to the challenge of limiting the discussion by determining a beginning and an end. As we are historians, there will be a chronological aspect to this focus, as we must place the research in time; similarly, we need to limit in most cases the geographical or spatial boundaries of the question. Here, the old traditions mentioned in the previous chapter of dividing the past into chunks of time and space continue to operate. What will soon become obvious is how difficult these decisions are. How much previous information is needed to provide an appropriate context for the subject under consideration? Where does your analysis end, and how much effort should be placed on the long-term implications and consequences of the problem you have identified? These are not easy issues to resolve and much of the discipline required in the writing of history is driven by addressing them. What matters is how you see the problem coming into focus and how much attention you wish to place on what follows from your question. In some cases, this will not be an issue at all; but in most there will be the decision of whether to add a brief prologue or epilogue or substantial chapters at the beginning or end. What matters is your contract with the reader, an understanding usually implied in the introduction to your own research, defining your own contribution to the historical debate.

Where you place the contract with your audience is really a function of how you structure your work. In some instances, this will appear in a preface or a brief chapter entitled 'Introduction'. In other examples, it can be incorporated into an exhaustive 'state of the question', as you explain in detail what you intend to prove and how and why your analysis is different and your conclusions significant. There is no template to the writing of history: each historian must follow the imperatives of a chosen methodology, the evidence structure, and the historian's personal style.

The Contract with your Audience

This contract with the reader is really straightforward, even if it is often hidden among various other considerations. You have established the issue you intend to address – the question – and where this question currently sits in the received scholarship. You now must clearly state what your contribution will be and how you intend to prove it and why it matters. In this, you will usually discuss what archives, sources, and other kinds of evidence you intend to employ; you will review your method, describing the kind of historical research you are doing – for example, political, social, economic, intellectual – and the lens that you intend to use – feminist, queer, Marxist, and so on. Your reader should know from the beginnings the assumptions you have made and how your work will develop; to do this, a historian needs to be frank and clear about these issues. This is not to say that any of these categories is rigid and closed. Any good historian will use the tools of many forms of historical evidence and writing to illuminate the past; but all of us have a fundamental perspective which will shape the work as a whole.

For example, let's return to the example of the murder of Alessandro de' Medici in 1537. You have stated your own position, the thesis you intend to develop and prove, how this differs from what others have done and identified the sources you intend to use. Now, you need to indicate that your motive falls mostly into the category of, for example, Political History: how did the murder result from and shape the political history of Florence? You might also indicate that there is a social element by discussing the still fluid elements of elite aristocratic culture in the former republic of Florence and which popular assumptions of policy and behaviour were affected by this inchoate vision of royal authority. You can admit to some issues of race in the murder, and in the popular and elite reaction to Alessandro's character and actions. Queer theory might lead to some elements of why the two cousins were initially so very intimate and then fell into lethal discord. And, then, perhaps Women's History or a feminist perspective might be applied to explain the two men's misogynistic behaviour and the plot to rape a shared young female relative. In other words, you may have a primary purpose – the political development of Florence between 1530 and 1550 – but the analysis must be multifaceted to be a satisfying study.

Structure

The overall structure of the body of the work will largely follow these methods but also almost invariably be chronological in organization. Historical works are difficult to pry away from chronology, as we are looking at change over time and we see time in chronological sequence. Also, we look for the causes and consequences of actions: these, too fit best into a linear analysis. And, finally, there is clarity and coherence.

Moments in the past – even a brief one like that event in 1537 – will have a large cast of characters, a great deal of contextual information, and a deep analysis predicated on exhaustive research. To achieve success in your writing, then, it is important to have a structure that elucidates rather than obfuscates your work. Experimentation with the reader's expectations works extremely well in fiction and film: it really does not work in history. You do need to hold your reader's interest, but this should be through effective prose and satisfying insight, not stylistic tricks.

A Conclusion

The conclusion of your research needs to be clearly identified as such. If you established a contract with your audience in the introduction, now you need to indicate clearly that you have fulfilled your part of that contract. The results of your research represented by your unique and significant contribution to scholarship on the question you initially identified must be made clearly manifest. The conclusion should reflect in mirror image the introductory elements described when you made your intentions known. Equally, you need to highlight what you consider the most important of your conclusions and what new insights they contain. Setting a hierarchy of results is not a weak stylistic whimper of a conclusion but a realistic recognition that there are some very important results from your work and others that are not as significant, at least in the context of the question you set for yourself. Others might pursue these secondary results, believing you had missed the point; but that is their work, not yours. All conclusions in historical research are not of equal radiance in the galaxy of ideas. Put forward your strongest contributions first and let the others follow.

Bibliographies and Notes

Next, it is required of you to record where your evidence came from: all serious works of history must have a bibliography, ideally divided into primary and secondary materials and these into unpublished documents and works in print. You must be scrupulous in the extreme in your bibliography, especially as modern instruments of scholarly notation do not always require a full bibliographical entry in your footnotes or endnotes. If you are using a historical archive, be exact in where the documents from that archive are found so that others can locate them. Give precise information as to which works in your bibliography are translations, with the translator noted, as many a devil escapes from the poor rendering of foreign prose. Indicate any information you received by privileged, unique correspondence, as often this is extremely important, especially in contemporary historical research, but very difficult to corroborate. If you claim to have secret information which cannot be identified, your authority evaporates, as this is beyond verification.

Because your research required investigation of materials – both primary and secondary – in languages other than English, quotations or pieces of evidence from these studies or documents must be translated in the body of your work. Unless your audience is extremely narrow, you must assume that your reader will need a translation: this is both useful, as it allows your analysis to progress seamlessly, and courteous: no one likes confronting material they cannot read. The general convention now is to put the English translation within the continuous prose of your discussion; however, it is necessary to include the original, in its original language and format, in the notes. There must be an opportunity for your reader to assess the accuracy of your translation. The reason the format should be reproduced results from the important information revealed by how evidence is organized on the page. It might not be convenient but it is part of your contract with your audience.

The same is true for technical, difficult, or archaic usages. History texts have a habit of migrating beyond a narrow audience of specialists. Consequently, keep in mind that your work might be of interest to those in other disciplines or outside your core readership of scholars. So, define terms that your immediate colleagues would know but not all historians, let alone members of the general public. Modernize archaisms, either in notes or in square brackets in the text. Expand abbreviations, especially in medieval and early modern documents where this is an absolute necessity. Again, this is best done with square brackets or even italics, because your expansions must be clearly indicated. In fact, if there are many of these, provide an abbreviation legend at the beginning to ensure consistency. Note variant readings, if two of your documents seem to disagree; and be certain to indicate where you are filling in missing material from the document. In early documents, the ravages of time have erased script. To a skilled historian of the period, the meaning or intention of the author is often obvious, but you still must indicate when you are substituting your readings for lost originals.

Maps and Illustrations

What else do you need in an effective work of history? Because we have limited our research in space, maps are useful to clarify exactly what you mean. Place names change over time and entire communities migrate. So, give your reader visual evidence through clearly drawn maps. If you need graphs or charts, include them in the body of the work where they will be most useful. Gathering all such instruments at the end of the work might be efficient for the printer but not useful for the reader. And, be sure that the sophistication of the graphs and charts are consonant with the level of the research. If you are writing for a highly specialized audience, it is fair to provide complex charts, graphs, and other materials; if your hope is to reach a wider public, then be sure that this information is easy to understand and interpret. This pertains not only to the design of the graphs or charts but to the legend explaining how to interpret them. Be clear and never assume your reader will understand anything that is not obvious.

Images – pictures – are a central element in many works of history. If the genre is the study of Cultural History, this is even truer. What is important to remember is that images are evidence and must be used with the same rigour and clarity as any other piece of evidence. Choosing images is a major investment in time, as only the best examples should appear and only those that add something to the reader's understanding of the work. Gratuitous images are often entertaining but they are not of much value. So, you must ask yourself, for example, whether it is important to know what a historical character looked like. Does his or her appearance matter? Is there a portrait that illustrates his or her rank, taste, style of life, age, family, environment or any other pertinent fact? If so, use it; if not ask whether you might not fill that space with something else. Think of the example of Alessandro de'Medici: his African features were very pronounced and often remarked upon, so a portrait is significant. Visual understanding and Visual History are exceptionally important in any reader's appreciation of the past. You cannot assume that your reader has been to Florence, so add an image of where an event occurred so that the imagination of the reader can put that distant moment in time into the memory theatre that emerges from all reading. What did a bedroom in a patrician palace in Florence in 1537 look like? Because this is useful in understanding the murder of Alessandro, add a photo from a museum like the Museum of the Florentine House (Palazzo Davanzati). Remember that the past is a foreign land and you need to display how local customs and colour operated in that distant place.

If the subject of your history contains constant references to royal houses or dynasties, a genealogical chart can be useful because it avoids the complex verbosity of who begat whom and when. Also, lists of prime ministers, presidents, or popes can help in giving your readers a quick index of information. These tools tend to be most effective in textbooks or more popular histories: it is assumed that specialists know these things from experience and close reading in the discipline. But what is stressed here is that the historian has the obligation to think of his or her audience: what can be assumed, what needs to be clearly listed and how the information in the text can be made more accessible.

Envoi

The writing of history, then, is not a task like any other. Rather, it is a highly professional enterprise with clearly defined objectives and conventional assumptions. As with any academic undertaking, it requires a great deal of preliminary organization and thought. The research in archives, libraries, and special collections really constitutes the second stage of work, after the question has been defined and the review of the received scholarship – the state of the question – determined. The work of research in original documentation is an exacting and demanding occupation that presupposes highly specialized skills in bibliography, research, palaeography, organization, argument, editing and judgment. It is hardly for the faint of heart. But these skills, together with an engaging prose style, can turn a work of history into more than another text directed towards a learned audience of the author's peers. It can be an important insight into how the past operated and provided a platform for future developments. It can be an adventure narrative or an expository report. It can be a biography of an influential man or woman or it can take a broad sweep of the past that integrates it with the experience of the present. It can be a detailed investigation into a small moment of our shared experience from which we can draw understanding or inspiration. The writing of history, then, is hardly just for and by historians. History is the record of our collective memory and as a consequence needs to be appreciated as exactly that; and ideally it should be sufficiently accessible that every educated reader can learn from its content and style. We all in some ways make history merely by living in the world and leaving records of our lives. We observe history as the current memory of those who went before whenever we walk down a city street, read a book, or see a picture or film. History is not separate from who we are and what we do in our daily lives; history explains how we got to be where we are and who we are. This chapter has described and analysed the work of professional historians; the next will speak to the historian in all of us.

8

Experiencing History

This book has discussed the elements that contribute to history and engage the historian. I have discussed the fundamental material of the historian's trade, such as evidence, method, argument, and audience. What I wish to do now is to discuss the history around us, how each and every one of us will contribute to the writing of tomorrow's history, even if tangentially, and how merely living in the world is a lesson in the heritage and memory of the past.

History Around Us

In the introduction to this book, I described the personal history illustrated by my relationship to my house and the family who lived there for so many years. This was an example to show that history is all around us, even in our private spaces, where the intersection of family, place and memory creates a narrative that gives a deeper meaning to daily life. History is not confined to university classrooms, libraries, TV speciality channels, and antiquarian societies: it is everywhere because it is the foundation of who we are in every aspect of our lives. To recognize this simple but profound reality, I would like to suggest that we all participate as historians just by walking along the streets of our city or town, or, perhaps, the grand avenues or medieval warrens of

The Experience of History, First Edition. Kenneth Bartlett.

European cities where a very long history is built right into the bricks and mortar of the urban landscape.

When exploring any built environment, think of it as evidence from the past and how that past interacts with the present and offers promise for the future. Let's do this, beginning in the centre of the town which is usually the oldest part, as urban space expands through concentric circles from the centre. What we see depends to a great degree on the age of the place: if the town or city is a recent foundation, some of my observations will not work; but if it is very old, the cityscape is more complex, a palimpsest of layers, one atop another requiring some imagination and knowledge to excavate. I'll assume an old town, simply because history is more evident, inasmuch as change over time is visible in so many ways.

Nevertheless, we must begin with a number of questions which arise when investigating built space as historical evidence. Why is the town or city here at all? Is it a port on a river, lake, or ocean? Is it a major railway junction or on a canal route? Is it an administrative centre, a seat of government for a region or a nation? Is it – or was it – a military post, offering protection and security in unstable times? Is it an economic centre, controlling the financial aspects of a broader territory? Is it a market town, serving an agricultural region, or it is it a manufacturing centre, with factories producing goods to be sold elsewhere, or a religious centre, attracting wealth and power from the faithful, or is it all of the above? This list is hardly definitive, as there are so many other categories of urban development, but I think the principle is clear. We must also ask how much of the original foundation is still there to be seen. Remember my comment that lost or negative evidence is still evidence; and the loss of a city's built history usually comprises part of its story. For example, was the original town built of wood, only to see those early buildings replaced with brick or stone as the community prospered and grew? Was there a terrible disaster that completely altered the shape of the historic centre, an event such as a terrible fire – as in London or Chicago – or an earthquake, such as the catastrophe that levelled much of southern Italy in 1693, leading to the rebuilding of entire cities? Was the city destroyed in war and rebuilt, like Ypres in Belgium after the First World War, or Berlin after the Second World War? Was the decision taken to modernize and make a city more visually coherent and grand for the purposes of celebrating a ruler or regime, as in Baron Haussmann's (1809–1891) rebuilding of central Paris under Napoleon III (*r.* 1852–1870)? Was there a major economic change that caused the city to grow very fast, changing it completely, as in the British industrial towns of Birmingham or Manchester, or the opposite, a decline in the local economy which resulted in a significant shrinking or even abandoning of sections of the city, as in Detroit, or any number of mining towns around the world?

Asking such questions can help explain the nature of the historic architecture and urban landscape and hence reveal the changes the town experienced over time. If the downtown has grand buildings that date over many centuries, then the site was important for that long span of years: an example of this would be Mexico City, which was a great capital from Aztec to modern times. On the other hand, if the entire urban structure is obviously recent and clearly of an age, like Brasilia, the purpose-built new capital of Brazil, a completely new town has been constructed for particular reasons. Then, look about at the greatest and oldest buildings in the historical centre. What are – or were – these? For instance, grand administrative buildings, royal palaces, imposing churches, and patrician palaces reveal a concentration of power around the seat of a monarch. These national showcase cities usually also contain broad avenues and open spaces for public celebrations and military parades, as well as splendid cultural complexes, such as opera houses, museums, and theatres; here, Vienna or St Petersburg are examples.

The history of cities in Europe emerges often from their oldest quarters. The usually extreme density of habitation still visible resulted from the need to maximize the use of space within the city walls. In medieval times and even later, the walls provided protection from bandits, marauding soldiers or war. The towns inside the walls were places of refuge and security, and even those born into serfdom could earn their freedom merely by living freely within those walls for a year and a day. Streets were narrow and dark, and buildings high. Land was expensive and class geography in these cities reflected the inhabitants' wealth not by separating economic groups by neighbourhood but by where they lived in a building. The wealthiest had their rooms on the second floor, above the shops at street level. The poorest lived at the very top in small spaces reached only by many flights of steep stairs and which were hot in the summer and cold in the winter. Social classes met on the stairs of the houses they shared, and were often mutually dependent, even worshipping in the same parish churches. The medieval or early modern city was much more integrated than the industrial metropolises that arose in the nineteenth century.

In our perambulations through our historic city, however, we need to compare these very old centres, which were usually walkable, with important structures close together in a densely inhabited space, with later, often nineteenth-century additions, such as suburbs, with reduced density, wider and straighter streets and greater distances between buildings. It is clear these areas predated the automobile, so we assume that the expansion of public transportation as a function of urban life made this more generous use of space possible. The wider streets allowed for first horse-drawn and then electric trams to convey workers to their jobs and back to houses that were made more comfortable through modern conveniences and healthier air. Underground subways later connected these concentrations of population in large cities like London, Paris, or New York; and the ability of a city to expand was assured.

Before those means of urban transport, however, there had to have been innovations in technology that allowed cities to expand so dramatically in size, especially the ability to supply them with sufficient, relatively cheap food. This presupposed improvements in national and international transportation: the railroads, paved highways, bridges and canals, and, most important of them all in some ways: the compound steamship engine that permitted enormous amounts of cheap grain to be shipped from North America, Australia, and elsewhere to cities in Europe, making hunger something that would subsequently result only from human policy rather than natural cycles. These same technological improvements allowed factories to operate anywhere, but usually in cities where labour could be concentrated and supplied, where raw materials could be transported on the same systems that brought food, and where the finished goods could be carried to markets around the world through modernized ports.

The concentration of labour and production in large cities attracted capital, that third necessity of capitalist production. Banks, stock exchanges, and commercial companies, not to speak of legal and accounting firms, were drawn to these metropolises, making the European cities of the nineteenth century amazing experiments in urban co-existence like nothing the world had seen before. City and town charters were granted, allowing for the formation of local governments to pave roads, provide safe drinking water, and remove sewage. Police forces kept order and municipal bylaws controlled what could be built where in an attempt to mitigate the dangers – indeed horrors – of many nineteenth-century towns and cities.

I am describing all of these details because such observations constitute the evidence of history. It is not only through the traditional investigation of documents that the past is revealed; it is made manifest in the material survivals from our past. This explains not only how cities grew but why so much of the European urban landscape is nineteenth century, the period of enormous expansion in every aspect of life. It explains the often decayed but once vibrant factories visible from railway carriages as travellers enter European cities: what is seen is what the railways engendered, the construction of that age of industrialization. So, the very shape of cities constitutes evidence, a form of proof of change over time, but change that occurred with such rapidity that every European government struggled merely to try to keep pace with what was happening. Technology and economics drove change in these places, and the urban landscape remains there to record it. It is not necessary, then, to enter archives or libraries to study history and become a historian: just go for a walk and observe, furnished with enough background knowledge to make sense of the visible evidence to draw conclusions about our own communities.

Social History emerges from our walks as well: plan an itinerary through the new neighbourhoods of the newly enriched, those still found in well preserved later eighteenth- and nineteenth-century districts. The mill owners and their overseers, the investors, bankers, lawyers, and successful merchants who catered to them wanted new and spacious dwellings. Often in Europe these were built in the west end of cities to ensure that the wind carried the soot and smell of the factories away from them. Look at the size and shape of the houses, large structures that presupposed a ready supply of cheap domestic labour. Look for the relationship of these neighbourhoods to parks, cultural complexes, and the seats of government and power: they are usually sufficiently close to connect those in power with those with money, education, and taste. This was the culture of the middle class and its reach was everywhere and its grip tight.

Now, travel to the other end of town to walk through the narrow streets of workers' cottages, the common two-up and two-down terraces of the industrial labourers and their fellows. These are close not to culture and power but to the factories and ports, the railroads, and the canals. Subsistence wages did not easily allow even for tram tickets: the expansion of the street railways and underground systems was for the middle class to get to their offices from their leafy suburbs. If possible, walk around to the back of these terraces and note where the toilets were – or still are – outside, behind the house. Look in vain for parks and greenery; these had to be sacrificed to maximize density to reduce cost. There will often be a working-man's club, operated by a trade union, church, or benevolent society – or occasionally provided by the employer as a kind of afterhours reward. See if there is a Mechanics' Institute, a place where industrial workers could improve themselves through education or training, something close to the Victorian moral heart. Note that the churches will often be quite different from those encountered in the middle-class suburbs; and in some instances, like England, even of a different denomination, as the owners and managers were Anglicans while their employees were Nonconformist, or, as they were called, chapel. Look for public baths where the poor could wash their bodies regularly; and look for taverns, as drink was one of the few releases from the drudgery of a laborious life. Compare the few shops you encounter with those you saw in the commercial streets of the middle-class neighbourhood. There was no demand for unnecessary or luxury goods, so in working-class neighbourhoods the shops will carry the necessities of life and little more.

Learning to 'read' a cityscape is one of the skills that all historians find useful, and one which amateur historians discover to be both compelling and enjoyable. The built environment can provide the context for all of the other elements of research that constitute the historian's craft. In general, these structures of material culture are becoming ever more significant in tracing change over time and represent in themselves so many historical approaches, as they simultaneously reveal evidence about Social, Economic, and Cultural History. Thus, other genres of research emerge as well from studying the physical remains of the past which survive as part of the built legacy of earlier times.

Museums and Art Galleries

While exploring towns and cities, more evidence can be collected from the obvious repositories of the collective experience of those who lived before us. Museums are obvious vehicles for preserving and discovering the past; and everything in them, especially if accompanied by professional, useful didactic panels, and labels, contributes evidence. Again, most of this documentation is from the material culture of the past; but the way that the objects are displayed, the explanations of what they are and their use and the context offered by the curators all clearly represent evidence. This is usually more immediate than a written record, as we can imagine the exhibit in our own lives, touching it, admiring its craftsmanship or clever design. Museum exhibitions, then, are very important parts of our appreciation of the past.

What about exact reproductions of original objects? Does a facsimile also constitute evidence? This is a central question for museologists and curators, first cousins to historians. There is an argument that something you can touch and use in a museum has a more engaging function than a priceless original in a glass case. But it is not original: it was made in our own times, which means that the original has been interpreted by modern hands. It also, of course, lacks the emotional appeal of knowing the original object was used by someone who lived centuries or even millennia ago. Here, as in so many of the judgments we have made in this book, the value of replicas resides in the purpose to which they are put. An analogy would be using a printed book containing historical documents which another historian has transcribed, punctuated, and expanded. If you need just the content and if you trust the transcription, that should be fine. But, if you building an argument that requires certainty that the document is in the autograph hand of a particular person, or was once bound with other materials or is dated according to the handwriting, the nature of the paper and ink and the formatting on the page, then the historian must see the original; a printed transcription will just not suffice. The same is true of objects. If you just wanted an idea of what a *sistrum*, or ancient sacred rattle, looked like, any image would do; but if you wish to argue that a particular *sistrum* in a museum was once held by a specific statue of a priestess of Isis, then you must search out the original.

Art galleries are equally important as repositories for material culture. Inside there are the pictures, sculptures, and decorative arts which reflect in their style and content the period in which they were produced. In itself this is so very useful, as we have a sense of what those people we study looked like, how they dressed, the character of their surroundings, and so much more. Our visual imagination is connected to our academic knowledge through art, and we gain an emotional association with a period that otherwise might be defined only through written documents. Here, too, as with the reading of a cityscape, it is necessary to learn to read the art. We must ask questions of it. First what is portrayed, by whom and for whom? In other words, the same kinds of questions I suggested we need to ask of written records? What level of society is represented and how do we know? Is conspicuous consumption seen positively or negatively? Do the female costumes indicate that women of high status did not – or could not – work, given the restrictions of their garments. Could these women even dress themselves in these costumes? Who else is in the picture: servants, family, mythological or political figures, children or some other image that can tell us about the society that created this art? Is the visual frame realistic or imaginary? Is the picture designed for public display or private use? When doing research of any kind we must get beneath the surface and ask probing questions of the surviving material. Be sure that this is applied to art as well as to documents.

Portraits have a particular attraction. We are all interested in people, and historians spend much of their working lives trying to understand the characters, motives, and circumstances of people long dead. If this is done only through archives, the human element can be lost. For example, Marie Antoinette of France (wife of Louis XVI, *r.* 1774–1792) was not a very effective queen, and she has suffered from a very negative press for centuries; but she appears as a very warm and attentive mother in those portraits of her with her children. The character she displayed as queen might have left much to be desired; but our impression of her as a woman, and, it was believed, the mother of a future king, result in a more balanced judgment. Of course royal portraits were constructed to be flattering, but we must ask who is being flattered and why. Images of people bring history alive, and it is for this reason in particular that biographies are illustrated; and, I would like to confess, as would we all, that the first thing I do when opening a biography is look through the illustrations sequentially to acquire a visual image of the period being studied, as it helps so much in our appreciation of the events of someone's life, to know what he or she looked like or how he or she aged.

Furthermore, all art is in some way propaganda. Art has an agenda, whether that of the subject, the artist, or the patron of the work. It is a narrative – even the most austere and stilted portrait of a woman or man in black. The purpose of the picture is to tell a story and locate a person, or event, in some context. As in letters, diaries, fiction, and even in much official documentation, there is an intention in a work of art to be realized; hence, it needs to be read with the same critical eye as a judicial or tax record. Indeed, trying to sort out the agenda often provides the opportunity for understanding the picture and how that picture functions as evidence. We investigate art, then, the same way we investigate any document from the past, with the same rigorous study. Similarly, the art historians, curators, or aesthetes who wrote about that work of art must be assessed exactly the way we assess other historians. They have their methods, ideologies, preconceptions, strengths, and weaknesses like any other scholar. So, in crossing the boundaries of discipline, we bring the same instruments of assessment into our reading as we do in the framing the state of the question in history. If we are writing history, this is the lens we use, although with sensitivity to the traditions and scholarship of other fields.

Decorative arts are also a very important source of historical evidence and one, like all other art forms, that provides both pleasure and insight. Objects that were either purely decorative or purely functional are somewhat easier to classify than those many artefacts that are both. Candelabra, furniture, porcelain dinner services, or silver serving dishes: all of these are both useful and often extremely expensive things that confer status, and function as advertisements of taste and connoisseurship. Because many of the decorative art objects in museums came from the personal homes of individual people in the past, they provide a particularly intimate insight into the characters and ambitions of the men and women who commissioned them or chose them carefully. Can we distinguish in such objects owners who were from new money or old? Do we see dynastic pride celebrated in the engraved armorial bearings? What materials are they made of and what can that tell us about the luxury markets at the time, or the skill of local as opposed to international craftsmen? Was the object an individual example, commissioned for one place by one patron, or was it available to others; and was it purchased together with a great many other things to furnish an entire house at one time or was it chosen to be a unique example of a beautiful and useful object? Clearly, the decorative arts have a special role to play for the historian engaged in understanding the entirety of the past, so those sections of museums and art galleries are particularly interesting spaces for research.

This chapter is about the experience of history, something we live with, see around us, and absorb into our investigation of the past or our personal lives. Cityscapes, architecture, painting, sculpture, and decorative arts provide easily accessible evidence for seeing how history is part of our collective memories, shared experiences, and visual imaginations. When confronting objects and images from the past we cannot help but to see ourselves from a wider perspective, to understand instinctively how those who went before us at other times and even in other places contributed to who we are at present. Also, by personalizing the study of history we recognize more powerfully how the constants of human existence are manifested in different ways, helping us to realize that certain things have always mattered fundamentally – family, status, security, and identification with a wider set of values, whether religious, ideological, or national – but that such things were articulated or interpreted differently in that far off country of the past.

History as Breaking News

Experiencing history is consequently part of our daily lives, whether we are fully aware of it or not. Besides the visual and cultural aspects of just walking through a city or town, or the common pastime of visiting museums and galleries, we become historians by following the news. In fact, journalism is often the first breath of history: the news matters and the news is history in the making.

How we follow the news is irrelevant. Traditional newspapers, online news feeds, television news channels, or news magazines all provide not only coverage of the day's events around the world but also usually add a measure of commentary. This corresponds closely to how we looked at the traditional writing of history by historians. The coverage in the news represents the evidence, accumulated by usually trained professionals with access to privileged sources; the commentary is like later historians offering interpretations as to what these events might mean, with varying degrees of depth and sophistication, depending on the audience. Moreover, a comprehensive newscast or newspaper will bring together a great many of the genres of history we discussed earlier. There are the political events, as well as the economic evidence of the day, such as stock market quotations, observations on the value of currency, or rates of unemployment; Social History appears either in the direct reportage of events in society but also as the human interest stories that regularly appear; and, Military History appears as well, as there are seldom days without conflict somewhere on earth. Some of the later iterations of the historian's craft will also emerge from particular stories covered. These can be stories related to Queer History in the coverage of, for example, the legal and social acceptance of same-sex marriage; or, Environmental History often emerges from the wide popular interest in climate change.

Because I did not include Sport History in my elaboration of many forms of historical writing, there is no need to expand the discussion by observing how sports broadcasts or news stories regularly place the achievements of an athlete or a team in the historical context of the sport, the event or the previous success of the team. Major international games, like the Olympics, are redolent with historical statistics, narratives, and parallels, extending not only to the late nineteenth century and Baron de Coubertin's (1865–1937) resurrection of the Olympic Games (1896) but to ancient Greece itself and the significance of athletic competitions that were so closely associated with the religion and society – even the politics and wars – of classical civilization.

Film and Television

Films and videos have become in their own right a form of historical narrative. The popularity of movies set in the past requires an exposition of the context of the action of the film so that the experience of the story is richer. All historical periods are represented in film, from prehistory to yesterday. Some attempt remarkable recreations of the past, with astounding verisimilitude made possible by computer generated or enhanced scenes; others are more fanciful, turning the past into a frame for what amounts to pure fiction. What I find most exciting about experiencing history through film is the immediate and profound effect it has on the audience. I noted that the observer of a picture in a gallery or an artefact in a museum must interpret the importance of the object through some knowledge of the period in which it was created, aided by the labels and didactic panels of the curators. But in film, much of this interpretation is done for you by the screenwriters and director; and the visual effects and the interpretation of the motives and character of historical figures become compelling. The screenwriters and director in this instance are acting like historians, taking evidence, offering various kinds of interpretation, and presenting a narrative of what might have happened, represented by characters from the past who drive the action. Because of the ubiquity of film and visual material in our contemporary world, what we saw on television or at the movies will shape our internal visions of moments in the past, regardless of the level of our academic sophistication. I, for example, simply marvelled at the set for the video series *Rome* (2005–2007) when I was given a tour of the lot of Cinecittà, the huge film production complex just outside Rome. The recreation both of the forum romanum and the plebeian houses of the Aventine was masterful, despite their not being to scale and not really in precisely the right physical relation to one another. I saw the care that was taken to make the grand temples and basilicas of the forum a somewhat reliable reproduction of what historians think they looked like, especially the use of vibrant colour on the façades. I also realized that what passes for verisimilitude and faithful reproduction of cityscapes in film is not the same as in professional historical research. The needs of the action of the film take precedence, and details are often sacrificed, if they do not add to the plot or characterization. For example, many of the Latin inscriptions were gibberish, while others in legible graffiti or displayed on the architraves of great buildings were quite correct.

Film and television, then, often with remarkable computer generated historical backgrounds, are the instruments that introduce people today to history. Of course, there are students who are required to master the traditional forms of historical research and writing; and there will always be those who will prefer the written word and allow their own imaginations to populate the narrative and provide appropriate bodies for the voices of the past. But we live in a highly visual world, with an entire generation now programmed to see pixilated images of whatever moment of the past they wish to enter. What has emerged is another source of historical narrative, indeed often an analysis that complements our highly visual approach to our experience of the past. The wondrous effect of using a computer program to walk in three dimensions through the Basilica Julia in Rome, or the cathedral of Florence or the palace of Versailles in France is an experience that historians cannot ignore. There is no point in declaring such innovations merely entertainment and not using them to illustrate a difficult point or to capture the imagination of young students who one day might be historians. This is not the same as sitting in an archive, transcribing original documents to be investigated, assessed, and employed in drawing conclusions about the past. But this is not to say that these electronic tools are not as important in their own way, provided that the intention of the programmer that designs them and the skill of the historian that employs them are as rigorously applied as in the archive and library.

Electronic Records, Social Media, and History

History is a living discipline, illustrated in my observation that we are all making history, living in history and experiencing history just by being conscious and alive in our own worlds. We are also the recorders of our own histories and lives in a way that would have been incomprehensible even a few generations ago. Almost everyone carries a phone that allows immediate comments on any number of events or experiences, something we have seen to be central to the historian's profession. Our phones are cameras which capture dozens of images every day, images that usually will be of significance just to the individuals involved and a small circle of friends. The ubiquitous 'selfie' has replaced the formal photograph and places everyone in the centre of his or her own narrative. Twitter, Facebook, and Instagram entries and any number of other technologies – and others not yet even invented – have completely changed the nature of evidence and the concept of research. We know minute, often intimate, details of the lives of millions of people, many of whom we have never met; and we can follow what their eyes have seen through the photos posted on websites around the world. We know their immediate responses to situations, whether these are the horrors of war or a lost cat; we feel the levels of indignation and personal commentary in a way that official records can never contain. Written diaries, which so often represent emotion recollected in tranquillity, have given way to tweets in which there is often much emotion but little tranquillity. There is little sober second thought in such social media, so using it as evidence is perplexing.

But that problem will likely never arise, as social media is ephemeral. It is deleted almost instantly in most cases and was meant to be read only once in a very specific context. There are no notes, references, or carefully constructed arguments: there is only immediacy. For so many obvious reasons, this evidence would be invaluable to historians writing not only about a particular individual but trying to gauge public opinion at a given moment in time or about a specific event; but this evidence vanishes, never to be used again. And, because photograph albums are now in the same classification as floppy disks or wax phonograph cylinders, the digital images we all now store on our computers and phones might not last unless they are diligently transferred, printed, or downloaded to some secure site. Our correspondence is by email, again ephemeral technology, meaning that future historians will never have the kinds of rich troves of letters produced by earlier historical figures. Think what we would have lost if the Paston family in fifteenth-century England, Madame de Sévigné in seventeenth-century France, or Charles Dickens in the nineteenth century had not preserved their correspondence! How much poorer our knowledge of their lives and their times would be!

This problem also applies to official documents. More and more of the records of our time are collected and stored digitally. As hardware and software technology changes, will these be kept? Indeed, at present records are more accessible on line and more easily read; but will they survive in sufficient series to ensure their usefulness in the future? Scholars are already having difficulty using electronic records of just a few decades ago because the machines needed to access and read them no longer exist; and too often the materials used for storage – especially on tape and certain kinds of disks – are being lost as the material decays. Furthermore, it is hard and expensive to keep such documents. Someone must either keep reproducing them in the most recent technology or provide machines to read the original. Add to this the vast increase in documentation, in part because of the ease of collecting and storing it in the short term, and the problems become apparent. For the sake of future historians, we all need to address the problem of electronic records management immediately.

These remarks are hardly a proscription of the technologies of the modern world. On the contrary, these offer an enormous opportunity to discover more about our generation than any other since we began to walk upright. We must, however, be wary and watchful, as we are talking about our grandchildren's ability to know us, as we know our grandparents. It is part of being human to want to have this information, as I suggested at the beginning of this chapter. The past cannot be escaped, because it is always with us, having formed the context of our lives and our collective as well as individual memories. As a living thing, then, history must adapt to new environments and use the tools, technologies, and achievements of all other disciplines and crafts to explicate the wonder of knowing where we came from. This has always been the case. As historians moved from clay tablets and cuneiform to papyrus to parchment to paper, the fundamental intention was to preserve the past and interpret its meaning in light of the present. When the *codex* (book) replaced the *rotulus* (scroll), it was very much easier to search the documents of received scholarship, facilitating the recording and reading of history. Gutenberg's printing press (1450s) eclipsed the manuscript book, with the result that ideas could be reproduced exactly so they could be challenged or accepted everywhere in the confidence that the community of scholars knew they were all talking about the same thing. The digitization of records and a great many printed books has permitted the search of evidence much more quickly and largely from anywhere. Although there will always be a need to see the original document, entire programmes of research can now be pursued online, as technology has become the most productive and efficient research assistant in the history of scholarship, which is why we must devise a mechanism to preserve these digital forms of evidence of our lives and build this into the practice of history. History has always been changed by innovations, technology, and new methods of analysis of the past; and historians always learnt to take full advantage of them. I said early in this book that history will always reflect the time in which the historian is writing; ours is no different.

History from Evidence on the Internet

Another consequence for historians of the digital universe is the explosion of material available on the internet that does not reflect legitimate records, reliable evidence, or professional research by trained historians. Personal opinion, biased – even bigoted – screeds, incorrect identifications, and shallow analysis all appear together with legitimate postings in the search results on any question you can imagine. Students in particular find discriminating between flawed internet material and legitimate evidence a particular challenge. We must remember that there are neither editors nor manuscript reviewers on the internet. Anyone can post anything with the result that extremely misleading documentation regularly appears in student essays and even occasionally in the work of historians who should know better. How are we to teach students and curious members of the community that such material must be handled with particular care? The answer lies in the methods and skills described already in this book in the sections dealing with print and manuscript material. Who is the author of the internet posting? What are his or her qualifications? When was the material collected, written or posted? Is it current? Through what auspices is the evidence made available or circulated? Does it arise from an official website, such as a government agency, university, or museum? Are there footnotes or references that allow you to assess the validity of the documentation? Is the entire document or article posted or just a selected portion, taken out of context? Because of the absence of professional gatekeepers and the proliferation of evidence from the internet, every user must exercise extreme caution in citing such sources as legitimate and corroborate any material by consulting reliable documentation. The internet is a wonderful, amazing and brilliant tool; but it can also often be a false friend whose advice must be tested.

Never before in human history have we as historians had so much access to so much information as today. Information, however, must be subject to careful analysis and tests, regardless where it originates. Students must beware of falling into the trap of easy research – which often leads to plagiarism – and must be confident in their sources. So, I counsel my students never to cite an internet source unless there are notes, a clear attribution of authorship, or manifest reliability, corroborating evidence for everything, including dates, and a quality of analysis, diction, and tone that reflects a professional rather than an amateur entry. This advice equally applies to images, one of technology's great gifts to history, as we are now able to see what we are studying, providing that dynamic visual imagination which adds so much vitality and colour to our work. I regularly teach an interdisciplinary undergraduate course on the city of Rome. I too often discover that my students' essays are illustrated with incorrect images, taken from the internet, usually originating with tourists posting their vacation photographs. Major structures are commonly misidentified in name, location, and date; where the tourist got this information I will never know, but the attributions are simply wrong. Consequently, students must find three images with the same identification. The specific image they choose is up to them; but they must be certain it is correct.

Because of the proliferation of internet and electronic sources, the work of the historian and what constitutes evidence will change and the amount of evidence available will be overwhelming, if this digital material is preserved. In many ways it will be wonderful: imagine if we had the tweets of the senators in Pompey's Theatre immediately after the assassination of Julius Caesar, or the reaction of Columbus's crew when they first set foot on the soil of the new world or their first contact with aboriginal peoples. I mentioned earlier that our historical narratives are usually observations recorded and reformulated in tranquillity, after – sometimes well after – the event. Immediacy offers a different perspective and one which can be invaluable. For example, it is painful to listen to those tragic messages from hi-jacked aircraft or from the World Trade Center, or even the eyewitness news commentators on that fateful day of 11 September, 2001; but those words provide the most powerful historical records of a day when the course of history changed. Everyone then mature enough to understand what was happening remembers where they were, how they felt, and how they reacted at that moment. If those messages are preserved, later generations will share that experience and immediately recognize that history is not only the record of events but of peoples' response to those events. Sadly, as in the case above, this often takes the form of a record of human tragedy, courage, and despair; but, later generations will be thankful to be granted the privilege of sharing a charged moment in our common humanity and a difficult insight into events that altered the course of world history.

9

Conclusion

We are All Historians

What I hope has emerged from this book is that history is not the compilation of 'facts' or the charting of some inevitable process leading to the fulfilment of an ideological or religious plan. Rather, history is the interpretation of how change occurred over time, based on the evidence that survives, the way that evidence is used and how others have assessed that process of change. The result is that there is no singular history to which we can all refer in the knowledge that we can agree to its conclusions and subscribe to its narrative. There are, in fact, as many histories as there are historians, as each new observer brings her or his own lens to the material of the past. This is no way to demean the conclusions of others, merely to state an obvious reality: historians will never altogether agree because each one of them is creating history itself in his or her unique research and writing. Furthermore, we, as students and readers of history, then add our own response to what we discover in books with historical subjects. We may choose to agree or disagree or we may focus on one element over another because we, as consumers of history, also have our agendas. I suggested in an early chapter that we must investigate the historian as well as the history and offered some questions that should be addressed to the author of any book we read. I am now in my conclusion proposing that you investigate your own motives as well. We all approach history with a set

The Experience of History, First Edition. Kenneth Bartlett.

of expectations, so it is naïve to believe that we as readers are only passive receivers of what we read. We clearly are not, as we use the contents of history books as evidence for our own projects, whether this is an undergraduate essay, a serious work of mature scholarship, or a popular survey of past events. When reading history we become historians.

I also described at some length how we experience history merely by walking down a street, reading a newspaper, watching a current events feed on our computers, or the network news on television. History is everywhere being made and we are the observers of this process, remarking on change as it happens, comparing it to what had happened previously and making judgments as to whether that change is for the better or worse. This is what historians do. The nature of the evidence is different and the investigation of the subject derivative and often superficial; but the process is essentially the same. In recognizing our role in making, experiencing, or 'doing' history, we acknowledge that the memories of the past and the collective experience of the present constitute a continuum that depends on our linking these elements into something like a coherent narrative. I am not suggesting a solipsistic universe where our own thoughts constitute the only historical reality: I am instead stating that evidence unseen, books unread, events unobserved, or places not experienced exist in a passive, indeed useless, way. Until the documents are found and read and the work of others evaluated, the past remains an inaccessible archive. However much we speculate on the nature of that past or imagine how it might have developed, the truth is we do not and cannot know anything about it with any confidence; nevertheless, we can engage in a dialogue with those who went before us and with those who have served as previous intermediaries in this process. But to do so with insight and attention requires knowledge and certain skills.

An example would be to compare how historians interpreted ancient Egyptian civilization before the early nineteenth century with Egyptology after the 1820s. The discovery of the Rosetta Stone in 1799 during Napoleon's Egyptian campaign permitted the French scholar Jean-Francois Champollion (1790–1832) to decipher for the first time Egyptian hieroglyphics because the stone recorded a decree in that ancient priestly script (hieroglyphics) as well as in Greek, and the demotic (popular) language. For the first time the surviving records of an entire civilization before the conquest of Egypt by Alexander the Great in the fourth century BC became available. With reliable evidence now in place what emerged was how ridiculous so many of the previous interpretations of Egyptian inscriptions had been and how much more we could learn about that civilization. Revolutions happen in history as in any other discipline or in life; and these moments of discovery often have the effect of overturning all of our assumptions about what we thought we knew about the past.

We are All Disciples of Descartes

When the French philosopher and mathematician, René Descartes, published his elegant little *Discourse on Method* in 1637, he established the foundations of what we today know as scientific method. Although history is hardly a science – despite the discipline's migration to social science faculties in some universities – it still follows Descartes' design for the assessment of knowledge and evidence. We, as historians, follow the lead of scientists in believing that we cannot accept anything as true until it has been proven to be true. For us this is an extremely important element because it reminds us not to fall into the trap of letting our desire to reach certain conclusions drive our analysis and our method. Whatever our beliefs or ideologies, we cannot succumb to making the evidence fit a predetermined conclusion: we must let the documents lead us wherever they will. Our method must be rigorous and our evidence carefully chosen to elucidate our subject. Although it is difficult, we must, like scientists, be as dispassionate as possible, if we truly desire to understand how change occurred in the past.

Furthermore, Descartes suggested that we must look at a problem not as an entirety; we should divide it into as many of its component parts as possible and address these smaller, simpler issues separately and reassemble the larger problem only at the end. Again, we understand this application in scientific research; but how does it pertain to history? In my chapter on the various genres of historical study and in my delineation of the various kinds of evidence available, I really am proposing exactly this Cartesian procedure. Historians should look at different kinds of documents separately, on their own terms, and then assemble them to bring together a coherent picture of the past. This is that mosaic – or jigsaw – methodology that applies in so many approaches to so many areas of research: rather than trying to imagine the entire complex picture as a whole, choose the small bits of the puzzle – the tesserae or jigsaw pieces – individually and place them where they fit until the entire picture becomes clear.

This is obvious in looking, for example, at economic documents in one part of a study and the cultural material in another, drawing them together only in the final conclusions when we integrate all of our findings into a comprehensive narrative. But it equally works in assessing the past from the many perspectives I outlined previously, taking advantage of the diverse methods and materials of the various ways of investigating the past. A modern historian seldom works in just one sub-discipline: this is to relinquish too many other opportunities to investigate the broader perspective of the past and permit other voices to speak. So, think of Descartes and his method when compiling our evidence and structuring our research. How many ways can we read the material? How many different kinds of documents are available? How can the complexity of the experience of those in the past be shown to parallel the complexity of our own lives in our modern world? Dividing the big question into its component parts will help both in actual research and in drawing more valid conclusions.

Remember my example of the assassination of Duke Alessandro de'Medici of Florence in 1537. I suggested that there could not be a single route to interpreting that one event: the variables were too many and the evidence too complex. So, it was imperative that everything we know about that murder almost five centuries ago be assessed to reach a conclusion that would satisfy our desire to understand such a strange event while not sacrificing any of the rigorous scholarship demanded of a modern historian. It is only in looking at that bizarre event from a great many perspectives can we ever hope to make a reasonable suggestion as to what happened and why.

My argument here is not that history can operate like a science. I think we have learnt that Karl Marx's belief that he had discovered the quasi-Newtonian laws of history was either vainglory or foolishness. Similarly, Auguste Comte did not reveal the workings of the mechanistic laws of society, although he did invent sociology; and any historian who believes that the future can be read through the tea leaves of the past or that history repeats itself or that we have reached the end of history is playing in the league of the delusional. What I am suggesting, however, is that an insight into how change happened over time in the past and the skilful use of available evidence and a rigorous method of investigation can produce very satisfying insights into why things are the way they are. History can help us understand why we live under the institutions we do, obey the law, behave in certain ways, or think in certain ways. History cannot foretell the future or even guide our actions in the present; but it can help us to understand who we are and how we got here. For that reason the study of history is the study of human experience, our collective, shared experience, forged into an accessible common memory. It must be done well, with care and rigour, and it must be respectful of those who have gone before and honour those who continue their legacy.

Some Final Words

There is, then, no singular answer to the question of the purpose of history. It is simultaneously a process, a skill set, and a learned discipline. It can be an antiquarian delight, giving simple yet profound pleasure from merely knowing interesting things. History can entertain at cocktail parties or dinner; it can be of service for the completion of crossword puzzles. But I hope this book has proved that it is much more. History is the common library of human experience, one in which each volume has a different author and written for a different audience, a collection of observations, documents, and survivals of times long past, with no reliable observer left to set the story straight. History is a journey into the unknown of the many public and intimate worlds we have lost; the past really is a different country, one whose language, customs, society, structures, currency and habits are impossible to fully acquire. As historians, we will, then, always be outsiders, looking in through a very dark glass; but what we see inside is a wonderful story of shared human experience and the contributions of the lives of others to the universe we currently and collectively inhabit. The past made us who we are, even if this is only who we think we are. It is therefore worth studying. In fact it is imperative that we have some understanding of the past just to ensure that our decisions and experiences today can enjoy greater depth and complexity. That said, to embark on this journey into the past we need to take precautions and understand both the nature of that adventure and guides that are available to help us reach our destinations. All of the skills required are those of a useful life, regardless of place, class, occupation, or origin. They are the foundations of the well trained mind, able to collect, assess, and communicate complex ideas from many kinds of evidence to draw useful conclusions. It is not a simple process, but the past is not an easy place to visit.

Suggestions for Further Reading

Appleby, J., Hunt, L., and Jacob, M. *Telling the Truth About History.* New York: W.W. Norton, 1994.

Arnold, J.H. *History: A Very Short Introduction.* Oxford: Oxford UP, 2000.

Berlin, I. *Historical Inevitability.* Oxford: Oxford UP, 1955.

Bloch, M. *The Historian's Craft.* New York: Random House, 1964.

Breisach, E. *Historiography: Ancient, Medieval and Modern.* Chicago: University of Chicago Press, 1995.

Burke, P. *The French Historical Revolution: The Annales School, 1929–2014* (2nd revised ed.). Stanford: Stanford UP, 2015.

Butterfield, H. *The Whig Interpretation of History.* New York: W.W. Norton, 1965.

Carr, E.H. *What is History?* Harmondsworth: Pelican Books, 1967.

Cheng, E. *Historiography: An Introductory Guide.* London and New York: Bloomsbury Academic, 2012.

Cohen, S. *Historical Culture: On the Recoding of an Academic Discipline.* Berkeley: University of California Press, 1986.

Collingwood, R.G. *The Idea of History* (rev. ed.). Oxford: Oxford UP, 1994.

Christian, D. *Maps of Time: An Introduction to Big History* (2nd ed.). Berkeley: University of California Press, 2011.

Daniels, R. *Studying History: How and Why* (2nd ed.). Englewood Cliffs, NJ: Prentice Hall, 1972.

Eley, G. *A Crooked Line: From Cultural History to the History of Society.* Ann Arbor: University of Michigan Press, 2005.

Evans, R.J. *In Defense of History.* New York: W.W. Norton, 2000.

Fischer, D.H. *Historians' Fallacies: Towards A Logic of Historical Thought.* New York: Harper and Row, 1970.

Gaddis, J.L. *The Landscape of History: How Historians Map the Past.* Oxford: Oxford UP, 2004.

Geertz, C. *The Interpretation of Cultures.* New York: Basic Books, 1977.

Gooch, G.P. *History and Historians in the Nineteenth Century.* London: Longman and Green, 1952.

Green, A. and Troup, K., eds. *The Houses of History: A Critical Reader in Twentieth-Century History and Theory.* New York: New York University Press, 1999.

Handlin, O. *Truth in History.* Cambridge, MA: Harvard UP, 1979.

History and Theory: Studies in the Philosophy of History (Journal).

Hoefferle, C. *The Essential Historiography Reader.* Cambridge: Pearson, 2010.

Howell, M. and Prevenier, W. *From Reliable Sources: An Introduction to Historical Methods.* Ithaca, NY: Cornell UP, 2001.

Hunt, L. *The New Cultural History: Studies on the History of Society and Culture.* Berkeley: University of California Press, 1989.

Iggers, G.G. *Historiography in the Twentieth Century: From Scientific Objectivity to Postmodern Challenge.* Middletown, CT: Wesleyan, 2005.

Jenkins, K. *Rethinking History* (3rd ed.). London: Routledge, 2003.

Kyvig, D. and Marty, M. *Nearby History: Exploring the Past Around You (American Association for State and Local History).* Lanham, MD: AltaMira Press, 2010.

Lévi-Strauss, C. *Myth and Meaning: Cracking the Code of Culture.* New York: Schocken Books, 1995.

Marincola, J. *Greek and Roman Historiography (Oxford Readings in Classical Studies).* Oxford: Oxford UP, 2011.

Novick, P. *The Noble Dream: The Objectivity Question and the American Historical Profession.* Cambridge: Cambridge UP, 1988.

Popkin, J.D. *From Herodotus to H-Net: The Story of Historiography.* Oxford: Oxford UP, 2015.

Powicke, M. *Modern Historians and the Study of History,* Westport, CT: Praeger, 1976.

Russell, B. *Understanding History and Other Essays.* New York: Wisdom Library, 1957.

Scott, J.W. *Gender and the Politics of History.* New York: Columbia UP, 1999.

Spengler, O. *The Decline of the West.* New York: Alfred A. Knopf, 1945.

Stern, F. *The Varieties of History from Voltaire to the Present.* New York: Random House, 1973.

Tosh, J. *Historians on History* (2nd ed.). London: Pearson-Longman, 2008.

Tosh, J. *The Pursuit of History: Aims, Methods and New Directions in the Study of History*, (6th ed.). London: Routledge, 2015.

Toynbee, A. *A Study of History, Abridged Edition of Vols I–VI*. Oxford: Oxford UP, 1987.

Wineberg, S. *Historical Thinking and Other Unnatural Acts: Charting the Future of Teaching the Past: Critical Perspectives On The Past*. Philadelphia: Temple University Press, 2001.

Woolf, D. *Global History of History* (rev. ed.). Cambridge: Cambridge University Press, 2011.

Index

Printed and bound by CPI Group (UK) Ltd, Croydon, CR0 4YY

09/06/2025

14686095-0005